JAMESTOWN EDUCATION

WORLD WORKS™

LEVEL H

TECHNOLOGY

FOOD

NATURE

McGraw Hill Glencoe

New York, New York Columbus, Ohio Chicago, Illinois Woodland Hills, California

JAMESTOWN EDUCATION

Glencoe

The McGraw·Hill Companies

Send all inquiries to:
Glencoe/McGraw-Hill
8787 Orion Place
Columbus, OH 43240-4027

ISBN: 978-0-07-878021-9
MHID: 0-07-878021-7

Printed in the United States of America.

1 2 3 4 5 6 7 8 9 10 066 11 10 09 08 07

Contents

To the Student v

How to Use This Book vi

Unit One TECHNOLOGY

1 **Computer-Generated Imagery** Seeing Is Believing 2

2 **Prosthetic Limbs**
Technology That Makes a Difference 14

3 **Television** Broadcast, Cable, and Satellite 26

Compare and Contrast 38

Unit Two FOOD

4 **Chocolate** Treat from a Tree 40

5 **Food Preservation** Keeping Good Food Good 52

6 **Organic Food** Nature's Way 64

Compare and Contrast 76

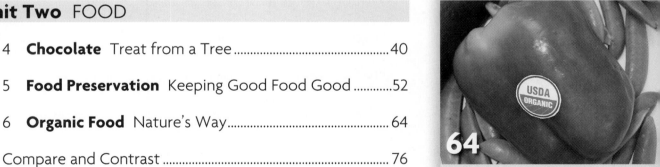

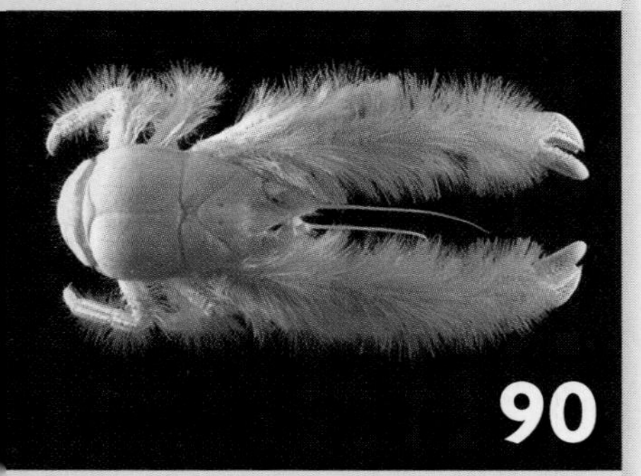

Unit Three NATURE

7 **Tsunamis** Force of Nature 78

8 **Hydrothermal Vents** A Dark, Mysterious World 90

9 **Parasites** Uninvited Guests 102

Compare and Contrast 114

Glossary 115

Pronunciation Guide 118

Writing Checklist 119

Progress Graph Instructions and Sample 120

Progress Graph 121

Image Credits 122

To the Student

This book has nine articles that explain how things work or how things are made. In Unit One, you'll read about technology. In Unit Two, you'll learn about food. And in Unit Three, you'll find out about nature.

The articles in this book will make you think. Some of the information in the text may amaze or even shock you. And each article is sure to improve your understanding of how the world works.

As you read this book, you will have the chance to practice six reading skills:

Visualizing
Finding the Main Idea
Summarizing
Making Connections
Asking Questions
Making Inferences

Each lesson in Unit One and Unit Two will focus on one of these reading skills. In Unit Three, each lesson will focus on several of the skills at once.

You will also complete reading comprehension, vocabulary, and writing activities. Many of the activities are similar to the ones on state and national tests. Completing the activities can help you get ready for tests you may have to take later.

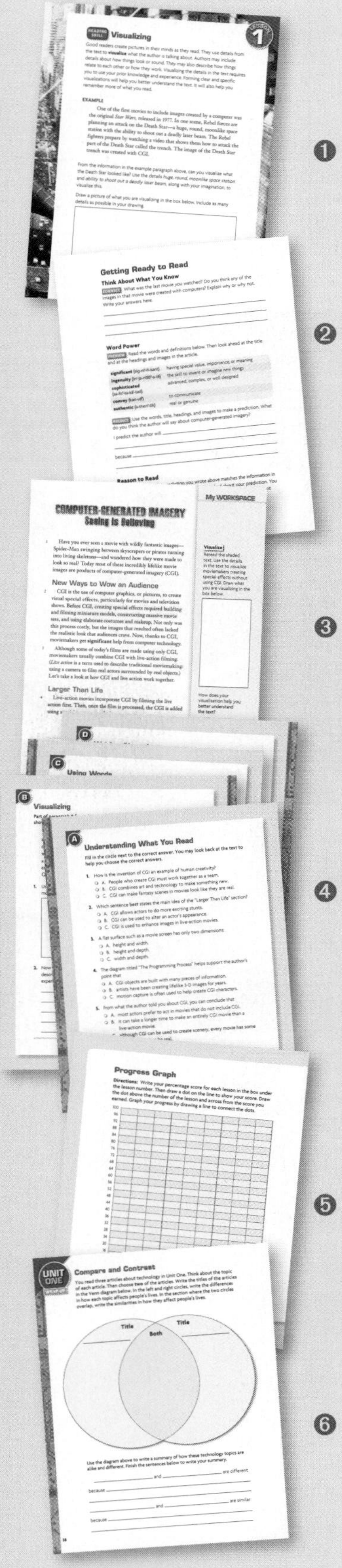

How to Use This Book

About the Book

This book has three units. Each unit has three lessons. Each lesson is built around an article about how something works or how something is made. All the articles have before-reading and after-reading activities.

Working Through Each Lesson

❶ **Reading Skill** Start each lesson by learning a reading skill and getting ready to use it.

❷ **Think About What You Know, Word Power, Reason to Read** Prepare to read the article by completing the activities on this page.

❸ **Article** Read about how something works or how something is made. Enjoy! The activities in the margins will remind you to use the reading skills.

❹ **Activities** Complete activities A, B, C, and D. Then check your work. Your teacher will give you an answer key to do this. Record the number of your correct answers for each activity. At the end of the lesson, add up your total score for activities A, B, and C. Then figure out your percentage score.

❺ **Progress Graph** Record your percentage score on the Progress Graph on page 121.

❻ **Compare and Contrast** Complete the Compare and Contrast activity at the end of each unit. The activity will help you see how the things you read about are alike and different.

Unit 1

Technology

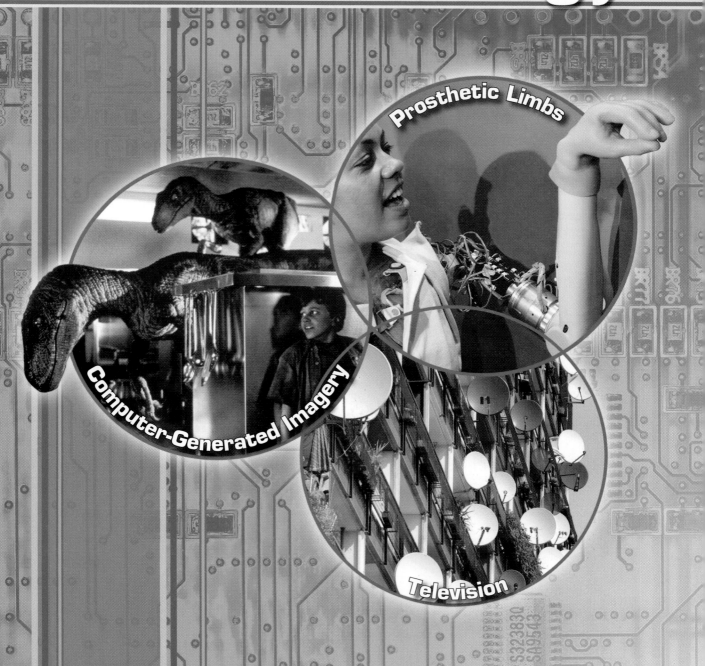

COMPUTER-GENERATED IMAGERY
Seeing Is Believing

CGI provides a new level of freedom for moviemakers and a new level of excitement for moviegoers.

LESSON 1

READING SKILL Visualizing

Good readers create pictures in their minds as they read. They use details from the text to **visualize** what the author is talking about. Authors may include details about how things look or sound. They may also describe how things relate to each other or how they work. Visualizing the details in the text requires you to use your prior knowledge and experience. Forming clear and specific visualizations will help you better understand the text. It will also help you remember more of what you read.

EXAMPLE

One of the first movies to include images created by a computer was the original *Star Wars*, released in 1977. In one scene, Rebel forces are planning an attack on the Death Star—a huge, round, moonlike space station with the ability to shoot out a deadly laser beam. The Rebel fighters prepare by watching a video that shows them how to attack the part of the Death Star called the trench. The image of the Death Star trench was created with CGI.

From the information in the example paragraph above, can you visualize what the Death Star looked like? Use the details *huge, round, moonlike space station* and *ability to shoot out a deadly laser beam,* along with your imagination, to visualize this.

Draw a picture of what you are visualizing in the box below. Include as many details as possible in your drawing.

Getting Ready to Read

Think About What You Know

CONNECT What was the last movie you watched? Do you think any of the images in that movie were created with computers? Explain why or why not. Write your answers here.

____

____

____

Word Power

PREVIEW Read the words and definitions below. Then look ahead at the title and at the headings and images in the article.

significant (sig-ni′-fi-kənt)	having special value, importance, or meaning
ingenuity (in′-jə-nōō′-ə-tē)	the skill to invent or imagine new things
sophisticated (sə-fis′-tə-kā′-təd)	advanced, complex, or well designed
convey (kən-vā′)	to communicate
authentic (ə-then′-tik)	real or genuine

PREDICT Use the words, title, headings, and images to make a prediction. What do you think the author will say about computer-generated imagery?

I predict the author will ____________________________

____

because ____________________________________

____

Reason to Read

Read to find out if the prediction you wrote above matches the information in the text. At the end of the article, you will be asked about your prediction. You will need to explain how your prediction is the same as the text or different from it.

COMPUTER-GENERATED IMAGERY
Seeing Is Believing

1 Have you ever seen a movie with wildly fantastic images—Spider-Man swinging between skyscrapers or pirates turning into living skeletons—and wondered how they were made to look so real? Today most of these incredibly lifelike movie images are products of computer-generated imagery (CGI).

New Ways to Wow an Audience

2 CGI is the use of computer graphics, or pictures, to create visual **special effects,** particularly for movies and television shows. Before CGI, creating special effects required building and filming miniature models, constructing massive movie sets, and using elaborate costumes and makeup. Not only was this process costly, but the images that resulted often lacked the realistic look that audiences crave. Now, thanks to CGI, moviemakers get **significant** help from computer technology.

3 Although some of today's films are made using only CGI, moviemakers usually combine CGI with live-action filming. (*Live action* is a term used to describe traditional moviemaking: using a camera to film real actors surrounded by real objects.) Let's take a look at how CGI and live action work together.

Larger Than Life

4 Live-action movies incorporate CGI by filming the live action first. Then, once the film is processed, the CGI is added using special computer techniques.

special effects (spe′-shəl-i-fekts′) images or sounds that are created artificially and included in a movie or television show to make it more believable and more enjoyable

My WORKSPACE

Visualize

Reread the shaded text. Use the details in the text to visualize moviemakers creating special effects without using CGI. Draw what you are visualizing in the box below.

How does your visualization help you better understand the text?

My WORKSPACE

Visualize

Reread **paragraph 6.** Use the details in the text to visualize what the author is describing.

What do you already know that helped you visualize this? Write your answer below.

____

____

____

____

____

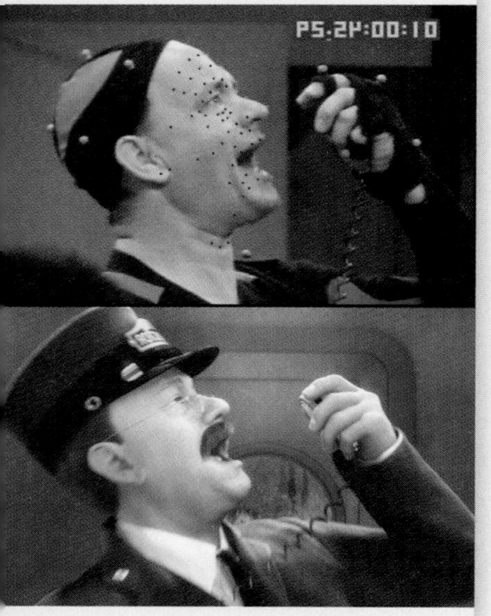

In *The Polar Express* (2004), the actors, including Tom Hanks, wore special sensors during filming. **Think about how these sensors helped the CGI artists create the final images for the movie.**

5 One of the basic ways CGI is used with live action is to enhance one or more aspects of an object or a character. For example, to create a scene that shows a burning building, the flames can be added with CGI after filming the scene. Or if a character has a special physical trait, CGI can be used to alter the actor's appearance. This was done in the 1994 movie *Forrest Gump:* an actor with two complete legs was made to look like a character (Lieutenant Dan) whose legs had been **amputated.**

6 CGI also allows actors to wear safety wires during filming so that they can do exciting and even dangerous stunts. Later the wires are easily removed from the film with CGI techniques.

Is It Live, or Is It CGI?

7 CGI can also be used to create an entire character or an entire location. In the case of a character, a real actor might play the character's role during filming, and then CGI experts later "paint out" the actor and "paint in" the CGI character. A computer technology called motion capture helps with this.

8 Motion capture involves placing special markers on an actor's body and face during filming. A computer program tracks the movements of the markers and records their positions at fractions of a second. So when it's time to paint the CGI character into the film, the artists have a record of the actor's exact body and facial motions to work from. For example, actor Andy Serkis provided the presence of the CGI creature Gollum during the filming of *The Lord of the Rings* trilogy. Although you never see Serkis's body in the movies, you do see his movements and facial expressions in Gollum's character. Motion capture can also help actors who find it difficult to act in a scene if the CGI characters aren't there at all.

9 Scenery is another movie element that might be created with CGI, especially if a movie takes place in an extreme location such as the open sea, a vast desert, or a deep jungle.

amputated (am′-pyə-tāt′-əd) cut off during an operation (usually refers to a person's or animal's legs, arms, fingers, or toes)

To create many of the battle scenes for *The Lord of the Rings* movies, first the actors in the foreground were filmed in front of a blue screen. Then a special CGI program was used to add the massive armies in the background. **Think about the role CGI played in making these movies more realistic and more enjoyable for viewers.**

The Illusion of Depth

10 So how do people use computers to create images that aren't modeled after real actors? It requires great **ingenuity** and a clear understanding of how our eyes see the natural world.

11 In the natural world, every object has three dimensions: height, width, and depth. But images on movie and television screens have only two dimensions: height and width. So moviemakers who use CGI must create the illusion of depth.

My WORKSPACE

Visualize

Reread **paragraph 11.** Use the details in the text to visualize a two-dimensional image and a three-dimensional object. Draw what you are visualizing in the box.

Now write a description of what you are visualizing. Be sure to describe **at least two** parts of your visualization that are not described in the text. These parts come from your own experience and imagination.

My WORKSPACE

Visualize

Reread the shaded text. Write **two** details from the text that help you visualize the 3-D images that skilled artists create.

1. ______________________

____

2. ______________________

____

What would you have to already know to be able to use these details to visualize?

____

____

____

____

____

12 Skilled artists such as painters have been creating lifelike three-dimensional (3-D) images on flat surfaces for hundreds of years—but their creations don't move. It's much more difficult to create 3-D images that not only move but also accurately mirror everything our eyes are accustomed to seeing in real life. It requires a team of talented people, including artists, scientists, and **computer programmers** who work with powerful computers and **sophisticated** software.

Get the Big Picture

13 The foundation of CGI is computer programming. Programming objects and characters to look and move realistically involves many pieces of information that build upon one another.

14 The first piece of information that the computer needs is the wireframe, which is a simple line drawing that shows an object's 3-D shape. Other programming instructions are then added to **convey** texture, color, and relationship to light, without which an object or a character won't cast the proper shadow.

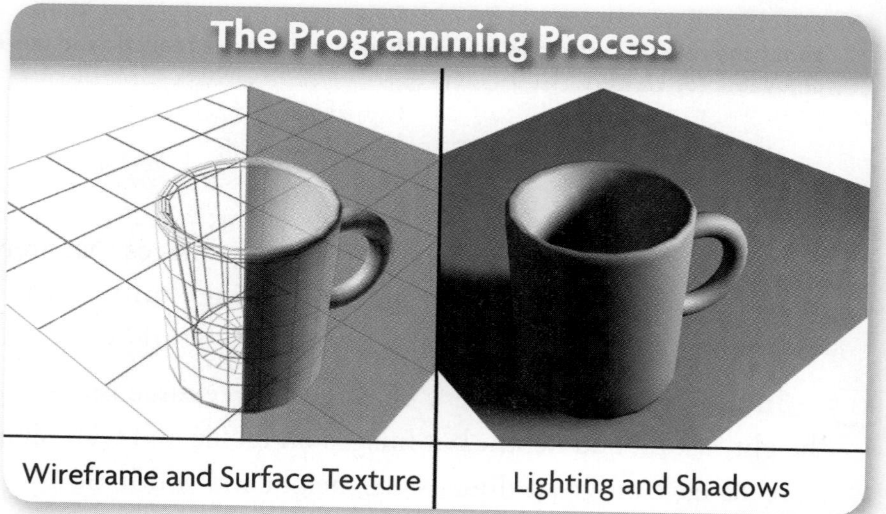

These images show how different layers of information, starting with the wireframe, are built into an object. **Think about how creating 3-D objects on a computer is different from drawing 3-D objects on paper or canvas.**

computer programmers (kəm-pyōō′-tər-prō′-gra′-mərz) people who use special computer languages to write instructions for computers

15 Further instructions are needed to determine a character's rules of movement. If a CGI character is supposed to have a humanlike appearance, his or her arms and legs must bend and rotate in ways that match the human anatomy. If they don't, a viewer's eyes will catch the inconsistency and immediately sense that the character is not **authentic.**

16 Sometimes CGI creators will use a combination of a wireframe model and motion capture. To create a scene that shows a CGI character walking across a room, first an actor wearing a formfitting suit with sensors on it performs this action while a computer program records the motion. Then the wireframe body of the CGI character is matched up with the recorded motion to create CGI movement that looks authentic.

No Small Task

17 Once the computer programmers have created instructions for each CGI character, a special bank of computers (sometimes more than 1,000 of them!) puts all the instructions together to create each scene. In some scenes, there is so much information to process that it can take several hours for even the fastest computers to produce just one frame of film. Because there can be more than 20 frames of film per second, it can take years to generate a full-length movie. *Monsters, Inc.* (2001), which was created entirely with CGI, took four years to generate.

18 Now that you know some of the secrets of CGI, the next time you see a movie with jaw-dropping visual effects you'll have an idea of what went on behind the scenes—and inside the computers.

Fun Facts

- 1970s: Moviemakers begin to use CGI.
- 1993: *Jurassic Park* integrates CGI and live actors with a level of visual realism that has never before been achieved.
- 1995: *Toy Story* becomes the first entirely CGI feature film.
- 2004: Motion-capture technology is used to create every character in *The Polar Express*.

My WORKSPACE

In this scene from *Deep Impact* (1998), CGI was used to create the image of a wave destroying a bridge. **Think about what CGI artists would need to know about the physical world to be able to create scenes like this one.**

Self-Check

Look back at the prediction you wrote on page 4.

- Does your prediction match the text? Why or why not?

Write your answers on a separate sheet of paper.

A

Understanding What You Read

Fill in the circle next to the correct answer. You may look back at the text to help you choose the correct answers.

1. How is the invention of CGI an example of human creativity?

❍ A. People who create CGI must work together as a team.
❍ B. CGI combines art and technology to make something new.
❍ C. CGI can make fantasy scenes in movies look like they are real.

2. Which sentence **best** states the main idea of the "Larger Than Life" section?

❍ A. CGI allows actors to do more exciting stunts.
❍ B. CGI can be used to alter an actor's appearance.
❍ C. CGI is used to enhance images in live-action movies.

3. Images on movie and television screens have only two dimensions:

❍ A. height and width.
❍ B. height and depth.
❍ C. width and depth.

4. The diagram titled "The Programming Process" helps support the author's point that

❍ A. CGI objects are built with many pieces of information.
❍ B. artists have been creating lifelike 3-D images for years.
❍ C. motion capture is often used to help create CGI characters.

5. From what the author told you about CGI, you can conclude that

❍ A. most actors prefer to act in movies that do not include CGI.
❍ B. it can take a longer time to make an entirely CGI movie than a live-action movie.
❍ C. although CGI can be used to create scenery, every movie has some scenery that must be real.

Score 4 points for each correct answer.

_________ /20 **Total Score: Activity A**

B

Visualizing

Part of paragraph 8 from the article is shown below. Read the text that is shown. Then use the text to complete the activities.

Motion capture involves placing special markers on an actor's body and face during filming. A computer program tracks the movements of the markers and records their positions at fractions of a second. So when it's time to paint the CGI character into the film, the artists have a record of the actor's exact body and facial motions to work from. For example, actor Andy Serkis provided the presence of the CGI creature Gollum during the filming of *The Lord of the Rings* trilogy.

1. Use the details from the text to help you visualize the process of using motion capture technology. Draw what you are visualizing in the box below.

2. Now write a detailed description of what you are visualizing. Be sure to describe **at least two** parts of your visualization that come from your own experience and imagination. Underline these parts of your description.

____

____

____

____

____

Score 5 points each for numbers 1 and 2.

_______ /10 **Total Score: Activity B**

C

Using Words

The words and phrases in the list below relate to the words in the box. Some words or phrases in the list are synonyms. They have the same meaning. Some words are antonyms. They have the opposite meaning. Write the related word from the box on each line. Use each word from the box **twice.**

significant	**ingenuity**	**sophisticated**
convey	**authentic**	

Synonyms

1. cleverness ______________________________

2. express ______________________________

3. highly developed ______________________________

4. true ______________________________

5. important ______________________________

Antonyms

6. crude ______________________________

7. minor ______________________________

8. inability ______________________________

9. withhold ______________________________

10. fake ______________________________

Score 2 points for each correct answer.

________ /20 **Total Score: Activity C**

D

Writing About It

Write a Postcard Suppose that after reading the CGI article, you saw a movie that featured CGI dinosaurs. Write a postcard to a friend. Tell your friend about the use of CGI in the movie. Finish the sentences below to write your postcard. Be sure your writing matches the information in the text. Use the checklist on page 119 to check your work.

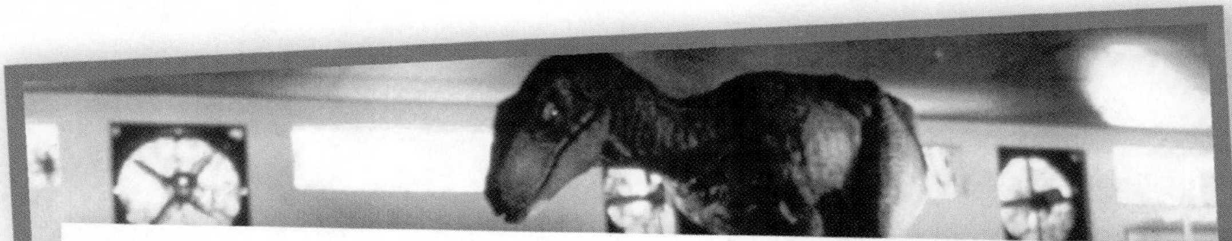

Dear ______________________

I saw a great dinosaur movie today. The dinosaurs were created with CGI. That means the moviemakers

____

____

But because there were people in the movie too, the moviemakers had to ______________________________

____

Did you know ______________________________

____

____

Sincerely,

____

____

123 T. Rex Lane
Anytown, State 54321

Lesson 1 Add your scores from activities A, B, and C to get your total score.

_______ **A** Understanding What You Read

_______ **B** Visualizing

_______ **C** Using Words

_______ **Total Score**

Multiply your **Total Score x 2** __________

This is your percentage score.

Record your percentage score on the graph on page 121.

PROSTHETIC LIMBS
Technology That Makes a Difference

People who use prosthetic (**präs-the′-tik**) limbs are able to do their regular daily activities and much more.

READING SKILL Finding the Main Idea and Details

The most important idea in a text is the **main idea.** The main idea is always a general idea. The supporting **details** are more specific. They give detailed information about the main idea. Good readers know how to infer, or determine, the main idea of the text when there isn't a topic sentence. To infer the main idea, study the details in the text to figure out what they have in common. Then use this information and your own knowledge to determine the main idea.

EXAMPLE

In 1993 model Heather Mills was hit by a police motorcycle while she was crossing a London street. The accident cut off her left leg below the knee. Mills was devastated by this loss, but she learned to walk with a prosthetic leg. Then she began to help others who had lost limbs. She collected 25,000 prosthetic limbs and shipped them to countries where land mine explosions have caused many people to lose their limbs.

The example paragraph does not have a topic sentence. The reader must use the details in the text to infer the main idea. Here are some of the important details in the example paragraph:

Part of Heather Mills's leg was cut off in an accident.

Mills learned to walk with a prosthetic leg.

She shipped 25,000 prosthetic limbs to people in other countries.

What do these details have in common? They all focus on Heather Mills and prosthetic limbs. Use this information to infer the main idea of the paragraph. Write the main idea below.

____

____

Explain how you determined your answer.

____

____

____

Getting Ready to Read

Think About What You Know

CONNECT What do you know about prosthetic limbs? What kinds of prosthetic limbs have you seen before? How do you think these replacement limbs work? Write your answers here.

____

____

____

Word Power

PREVIEW Read the words and definitions below. Then look ahead at the title and at the headings and images in the article.

interprets (in-tər′-prəts)	finds and understands the meaning of something
cumbersome (kəm′-bər-səm)	not easily managed or carried
precision (pri-si′-zhən)	the quality of being very accurate or exact
recipients (ri-si′-pē-ənts)	people who receive or take something that is given or offered to them
simultaneously (sī′-məl-tā′-nē-əs-lē)	at the same time

QUESTION Use the words, title, headings, and images to ask a question. What would you like to know about prosthetic limbs? Write your question on the lines below.

____

____

____

Reason to Read

Read to find out if the information in the text answers your question. At the end of the article, you will be asked to look back at your question. You will decide whether or not your question is answered in the text.

PROSTHETIC LIMBS
Technology That Makes a Difference

1 His goal wasn't to win the 2004 New York City Marathon—just to finish it. Less than 18 months earlier, Captain David Rozelle had lost his right foot and part of his leg in a land mine explosion while serving as an Army combat soldier in Iraq. But, like many others who have lost limbs, he refused to let his loss keep him from living a full life.

2 It took Captain Rozelle nearly seven hours to finish the grueling 26.2-mile race, but he made it—thanks to courage, determination, and his prosthetic limb.

On Your Feet Again

3 A prosthetic limb, or prosthesis, is a device a person wears to replace a missing arm or leg. Some people are missing limbs as the result of birth defects, while others lose limbs because of injury or disease.

4 Imagine doing your everyday activities without one or both of your arms or legs: opening a milk carton, carrying books, walking to class. For people who actually live this reality, a prosthetic limb can make a significant difference.

5 Most prosthetic limbs are made with plastics and lightweight metals, but the level of mechanical complexity differs between arms and legs. Legs are used primarily for one thing: walking. The human hand, however, produces thousands of unique movements, so the technology used in prosthetic arms is usually more complex.

My WORKSPACE

Visualize

Reread the shaded text. Use the details in the text to visualize Captain Rozelle running the marathon. Draw what you are visualizing in the box below.

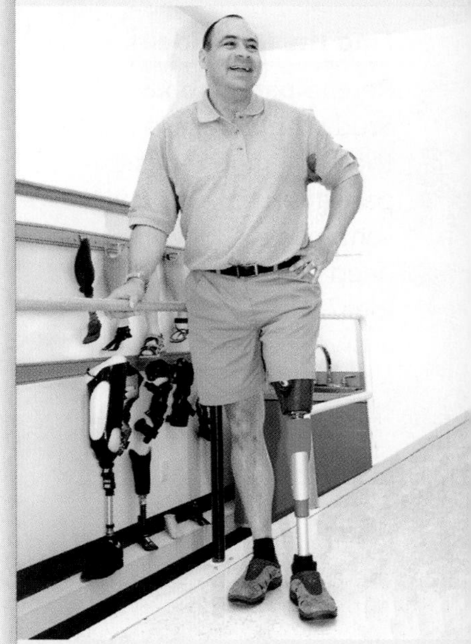

This man's prosthetic leg allows him to walk with relative ease. **Think about what he would need to do to get around if he didn't have a prosthetic leg.**

My WORKSPACE

Find the Main Idea

Reread **paragraph 8.** Study the details in the paragraph. Does this paragraph have a topic sentence, or do you need to infer the main idea? Write your answer below.

____

____

What is the main idea of the paragraph?

____

____

____

____

A Helping Hand

6 There are two main types of prosthetic arms. One is called a body-powered prosthesis because it's powered totally by body movements. It might consist of a hooklike device or an artificial hand attached to a cable that runs through the prosthesis. At the socket, the place where the prosthesis and the **residual limb** meet, the cable connects to an arm harness that is worn over the user's shoulders. When the user shrugs, that motion moves the harness, which pulls on the cable and closes the hook or hand. This is similar to the way squeezing a bicycle's hand brake causes the brakes to close around the tires.

7 The other type of prosthetic arm is externally powered, which means that a battery-powered motor generates movement in the hook or hand. The motor gets movement instructions from a **microprocessor** inside the prosthesis. Instead of being activated through a shoulder harness, it's activated through **sensors.** The microprocessor picks up signals from the sensors, **interprets** them, and then sends instructions to the motor about what movements to make.

8 Externally powered arms can have different types of sensors. Metal sensors called **electrodes** make direct contact with the skin and read myoelectric signals from the user's muscles. Myoelectric signals are electrical impulses that are generated whenever you flex your muscles. When the user tenses certain muscles in the residual limb, the sensors pick up these signals on the surface of the skin and translate them into movements, such as opening or closing the hook or artificial hand.

residual limb (ri-zi′-jə-wəl-lim′) the portion of a person's arm or leg that remains after the rest of it has been lost or removed

microprocessor (mī′-krō-prä′-se′-sər) a tiny computer chip that controls the actions inside a computer or computerlike device

sensors (sen′-sərz) devices that detect, or sense, a signal

electrodes (i-lek′-trōdz′) small wires or pieces of metal, usually used on a person's body, that carry electric signals

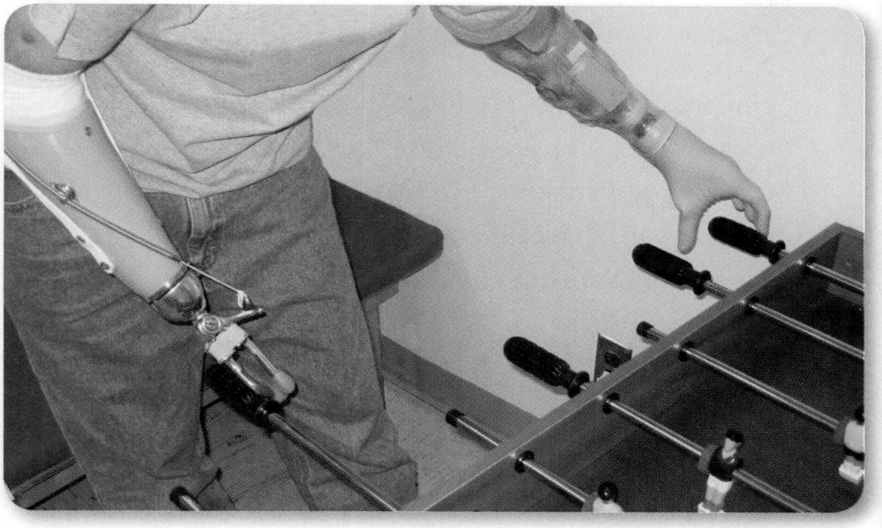

The man in this picture is using two different types of prosthetic arms. In this case, the arm with the hooklike device at its end is actually easier to use and more functional than the arm with the artificial hand. **Think about why someone might choose to have an arm with an artificial hand instead of a metal hook even if the hook works better.**

9 The type of prosthetic arm a user chooses depends on his or her specific circumstances. Body-powered prosthetic arms are much less expensive, easier to repair, and lighter in weight (partly because they don't contain batteries). Externally powered arms require less strength to operate and don't involve wearing a **cumbersome** harness. However, they do require the user to develop more precise control of his or her muscles to send the correct signals. Usually a team of doctors, physical therapists, and prosthetists (prosthetics specialists) will help pick the model that best suits a person.

Take the Next Step

10 Unlike prosthetic arms, most prosthetic legs are not powered at all. Prosthetic legs are built to provide strength and balance for walking as opposed to the **precision** that is needed in arms. The foot portion of most prosthetic legs is made of materials that bend under the weight of the individual's body to provide anklelike movement as he or she walks. When the prosthetic leg includes the knee joint, walking with a natural gait is much more difficult. This is because in many prosthetic legs, the knee must remain straight most of the time to avoid collapse. But new technologies are being developed that will allow the knee to flex safely.

My WORKSPACE

Find the Main Idea

Reread **paragraph 10.** Study the details in the paragraph. Does this paragraph have a topic sentence, or do you need to infer the main idea? Write your answer below.

____

____

What is the main idea of the paragraph?

____

____

____

____

Find the Main Idea

Reread **paragraph 13.** What is the main idea of the paragraph?

Explain how you determined your answer.

11 The prosthetic legs used by competitive runners like Shea Cowart (shown on page 14) don't resemble natural legs at all. These legs, which bend and then spring back to propel the runner forward, have allowed prosthetics users to run the 100-meter dash within about one second of the Olympic record!

A Learning Curve

12 Getting fitted for a prosthetic arm or leg is a complex process; the socket must be custom-made to fit snugly but comfortably around the residual limb. An exact permanent fit is particularly difficult for people with recent limb loss because residual limbs usually continue to atrophy, or shrink, for several months after surgery.

13 Once a person has a fitted prosthesis, it takes time to adjust to it both physically and emotionally. New **recipients** of a prosthetic arm or leg must get used to the physical size, shape, and weight of their device; they must also build strength and retrain their muscles. Simple movements such as picking up the newspaper, cutting food, climbing stairs, and getting out of bed must all be relearned. It normally takes from several months to a year for an individual to master the necessary skills.

Causes of Limb Loss in the United States, 1988–1996

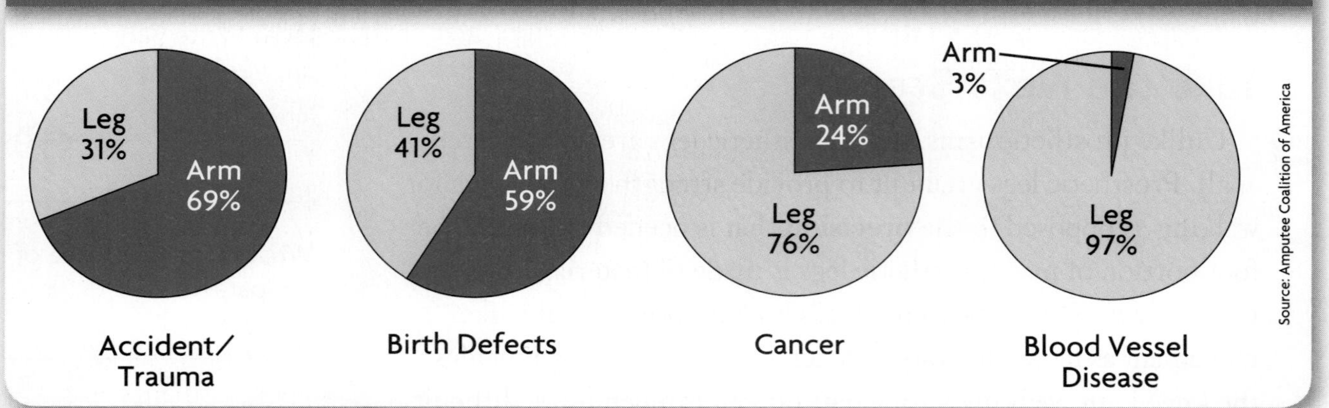

These pie charts represent the four most common causes of limb loss. Look at the pie chart for blood vessel disease. Loss of a leg due to blood vessel disease is often caused by diabetes. Look at the pie chart for accidents and trauma. **Think about why accidents would affect people's arms more often than their legs.**

14 Even after mastering these skills, a person might still struggle with anger, grief, or depression over the loss of his or her natural limb. Experts say the emotional pain of losing an arm or a leg can be compared to the pain of losing a loved one.

Keep Reaching

15 Although many of today's prosthetic limbs incorporate advanced technology, they do have their limitations. Take a moment to observe your own arm and the way you can swivel your wrist while **simultaneously** closing your fingers and straightening your elbow. As you can see, human arms can produce many movements at the same time; however, most prostheses produce only one movement at a time. To overcome this limitation, scientists are developing a new prosthetic arm that responds directly to thought control from the brain.

16 This new technology, sometimes called a "bionic arm," is similar to myoelectric arms in that it picks up electrical impulses from the body. But with the bionic arm, the user doesn't have to put as much concentration into creating movement. If the user has the intention to grab a doorknob, the bionic arm gets that signal from the brain and responds with simultaneous, fluid motions.

17 To be able to use a bionic arm, an individual must undergo a special nerve surgery to rewire the nerves from muscles that were amputated to certain other muscles that remain. Only a few people have been given bionic arms so far, but doctors hope to help more and more people over time.

18 Thanks to this wide variety of prosthetic technology, people like Captain Rozelle are setting inspirational examples for others by meeting life's challenges and staying in the race.

My WORKSPACE

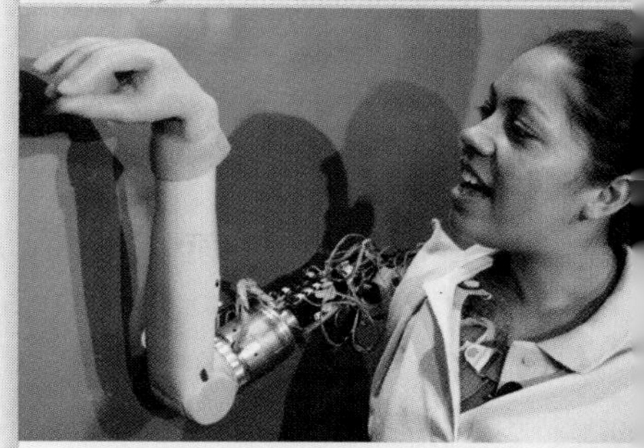

A bionic arm allows its user to move the hand, wrist, and elbow all at the same time. **Think about why bionic arms are especially helpful for people who, like Claudia Mitchell, have lost one or both of their arms above the elbow.**

Self-Check

Look back at the question you wrote on page 16.

- Does the information in the text answer your question? If it does, what is the answer? If it does not, where could you look to find more information?

Write your answers on a separate sheet of paper.

A

Understanding What You Read

Fill in the circle next to the correct answer. You may look back at the text to help you choose the correct answers.

1. How is Captain Rozelle an example of a leader?

❍ A. He did something that sets a positive example for others.
❍ B. He took nearly seven hours to complete a marathon.
❍ C. He lost part of his right leg in a land mine explosion.

2. Most prosthetic limbs are made

❍ A. with plastics and lightweight metals.
❍ B. to include many complex mechanical parts.
❍ C. so that they fit loosely around the residual limb.

3. One of the ways prosthetic legs are different from prosthetic arms is that only prosthetic legs

❍ A. must allow the user to do precise tasks.
❍ B. are designed primarily for strength and balance.
❍ C. rely on a battery-powered motor to create movement.

4. From the information in the pie chart titled "Causes of Limb Loss in the United States, 1988–1996," you can conclude that

❍ A. birth defects are the number-one cause of limb loss in the United States.
❍ B. the number of people who lost legs due to accidents increased between 1988 and 1996.
❍ C. people who have blood vessel disease are more likely to lose a leg than they are to lose an arm.

5. What problem is the invention of the "bionic arm" meant to solve?

❍ A. A person may experience feelings of grief and anger.
❍ B. Most prostheses produce just one movement at a time.
❍ C. Prosthetic arms can be very expensive and difficult to repair.

Score 4 points for each correct answer.

_________ /20 **Total Score: Activity A**

B

Finding the Main Idea and Details

Paragraph 15 from the article is shown below. Read the paragraph. Then use the paragraph to complete the activities.

Although many of today's prosthetic limbs incorporate advanced technology, they do have their limitations. Take a moment to observe your own arm and the way you can swivel your wrist while simultaneously closing your fingers and straightening your elbow. As you can see, human arms can produce many movements at the same time; however, most prostheses produce only one movement at a time. To overcome this limitation, scientists are developing a new prosthetic arm that responds directly to thought control from the brain.

1. Look for details in the paragraph that have something in common. Write **three** of these details on the lines below.

Detail ______________________________

Detail ______________________________

Detail ______________________________

2. Use the details you wrote to find the main idea of the paragraph. Write the main idea below. Then explain how you determined that this is the main idea.

Main Idea ______________________________

____

Explanation ______________________________

____

____

Score 5 points each for numbers 1 and 2.

______ /10 **Total Score: Activity B**

C

Using Words

Complete the analogies below by writing a word from the box on each line. Remember that in an analogy, the last two words or phrases must be related in the same way that the first two are related.

interprets	**cumbersome**	**precision**
recipients	**simultaneously**	

1. letters : reads :: signals : ______________________________

2. toaster : lightweight :: piano : ______________________________

3. questions : answers :: senders : ______________________________

4. with cheer : happily :: together : ______________________________

5. quickly : speed :: exactly : ______________________________

Choose one word from the box. Write a sentence using the word. Be sure to put at least one detail in your sentence. The detail should show that you understand what the word means.

6. ______________________________

____

Score 4 points for each correct answer in numbers 1–5.
(Do not score number 6.)

________ /20 **Total Score: Activity C**

D

Writing About It

Write a Comic Strip Write a comic strip about a person who is about to get a prosthetic arm. Finish the sentences in each bubble to write your comic strip. Be sure your writing matches the information in the text. Use the checklist on page 119 to check your work.

Now that my residual limb has healed, I'd like to ______ ______
PROSTHETICS LAB
There are several kinds of prosthetic arms. This one is ______ ______
How will I make it do what I want it to do?
There are sensors in the arm called electrodes that ______ ______
At first you'll have to practice a lot so that ______ ______
I'm willing to practice, because ______ ______
SEVERAL WEEKS LATER

Lesson 2 Add your scores from activities A, B, and C to get your total score.

______ **A** Understanding What You Read

______ **B** Finding the Main Idea and Details

______ **C** Using Words

______ **Total Score**

Multiply your **Total Score x 2** ______

This is your percentage score.

Record your percentage score on the graph on page 121.

TELEVISION
Broadcast, Cable, and Satellite

Today television viewers can choose from a variety of technologies and providers.

READING SKILL Summarizing

A **summary** is a shortened version of a text that includes key words from the text and your own words. A summary includes only the most important ideas from the text. When you read, look for key words and phrases that explain *who, what, when, where, why,* and *how.* These key words will help you find the most important ideas. A summary should be about 20 words or less and should be easy for someone to understand.

EXAMPLE

The First Television Shows

In 1939, at the New York World's Fair, the National Broadcasting Company (NBC) introduced a new communication technology to the American people. It was called broadcast television. NBC also announced that it would begin broadcasting two hours of television per week. Within a year, 23 broadcast television stations had been created.

One of the first popular television shows was a drama called *Faraway Hill.* Shows like *Faraway Hill* would later become known as "soap operas." Other popular programs of the time included Bugs Bunny cartoons and quiz shows.

Here is what a summary diagram might look like for the section of text shown above. The most important ideas are shown in the top boxes. The summary belongs in the bottom box. Use the most important ideas to write a summary of the example text.

Broadcast television was introduced in 1939 by NBC.	Within a year, 23 broadcast television stations had been created.	At that time, popular shows included soap operas, cartoons, and quiz shows.

Getting Ready to Read

Think About What You Know

CONNECT Think about television. What do you know about the differences between broadcast television, cable television, and satellite television? Which type of television is most familiar to you? Write your answers here.

___

___

___

Word Power

PREVIEW Read the words and definitions below. Then look ahead at the title and at the headings and images in the article.

motivated (mō′-tə-vāt′-əd)	inspired someone or something to take action
situated (si′-chə-wāt′-əd)	located in a specific place
array (ə-rā′)	a group of things that is impressive because of its size, quality, or variety
intrinsic (in-trin′-zik)	being part of the essential nature of something
ingenious (in-jēn′-yəs)	very clever; very good at inventing new things

PREDICT Use the words, title, headings, and images to make a prediction. What do you think the author will say about television?

I predict the author will ___

___

because ___

___

Reason to Read

Read to find out if the prediction you wrote above matches the information in the text. At the end of the article, you will be asked about your prediction. You will need to explain how your prediction is the same as the text or different from it.

TELEVISION
Broadcast, Cable, and Satellite

1 Think about the last time you watched television. Where were the television signals coming from? And did they come through an antenna, a cable along the wall, or a satellite dish? If you've ever wondered about these different television systems, here's your opportunity to learn more about them.

The Original

2 Broadcast television first became popular in the 1940s. Today it operates basically the same way it did back then: sounds and images from live or recorded programs are converted into electronic signals and broadcasted to the general public over radio waves.

3 Broadcast television stations use powerful sending towers to transmit their programs. The viewer's television set picks up the radio waves through an antenna (either small "rabbit ears" on the television or a larger antenna on the roof) wired to the set and converts them back into the original sounds and images.

4 The problem with broadcast television has to do with the way radio waves work. Radio waves can travel through the air only in a straight line, and although obstacles such as trees and buildings don't interfere with them, the radio waves can't penetrate landforms. This means that hills, ridges, and mountains block the signals. And even if the land is completely flat, the curvature of Earth itself begins to block the signals once they're about 30 miles (48 km) from the sending tower.

My WORKSPACE

Summarize

Reread **paragraph 4**. Find the important ideas by looking for key words and phrases that answer the questions *who, what, when, where, why,* and *how*. Write the key words and phrases here.

____

____

____

____

Use the key words and phrases to write a summary of the paragraph. Remember that your summary should be about 20 words or less.

____

____

____

____

____

My WORKSPACE

Visualize

Reread **paragraph 6.** Use the details in the text to visualize the Pennsylvania community setting up its cable network. Draw what you are visualizing in the box below.

What do you already know that helped you visualize this? Write your answer below.

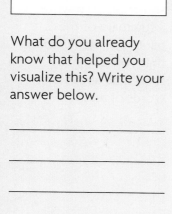

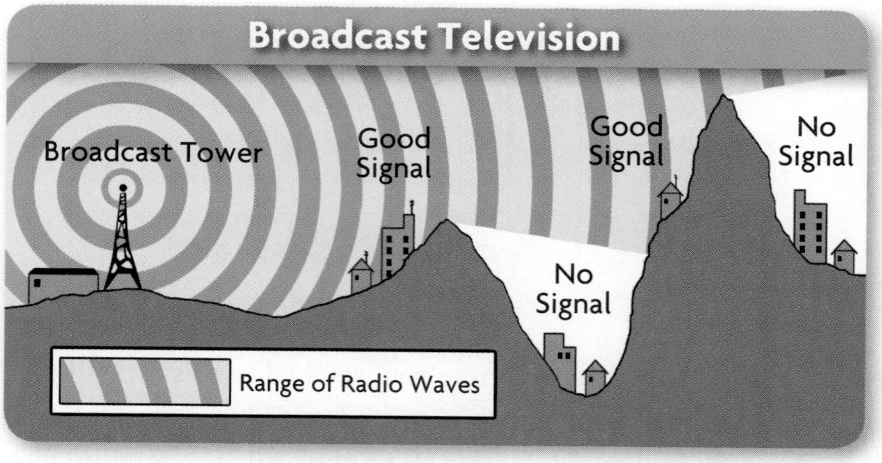

This diagram shows how landforms block radio waves sent from television stations. **Think about how the range of these radio waves would change if the broadcast tower were placed on top of the tallest hill.**

5 If you live on high ground or close to a sending tower, broadcast television should work very well for you. However, in less populated places, or where the land is low or hilly, all you will see on your television set is a blank screen. This limitation **motivated** people to search for another option, which led to the invention of cable television.

Here Comes Cable!

6 The idea for cable television came from a community **situated** in a rural Pennsylvania valley that could not get television reception. In 1948 they solved this problem by erecting a large receiving antenna on a ridge above the valley. Because the antenna stood on high ground, it easily picked up the radio waves from broadcast television stations. Then, using long cables resembling wires used to carry electricity, the residents connected the antenna to their individual television sets. This allowed the radio waves to travel uninterrupted from the antenna, through the cables, and into the television sets.

7 Soon other communities and some businesses started putting up antennas and creating both aboveground and underground cable systems, and the cable television industry took off.

More Choices, More Channels

8 Today more than 65 million U.S. homes have cable television. One thing that has boosted cable's popularity is the fact that cable companies can offer viewers a wide **array** of programs from stations all across the country—and even the world.

9 Most cable companies don't create the programs you watch. Instead, they operate as **brokers.** They negotiate contracts with the individual stations or networks that create the programs. The number of stations your cable company contracts with determines how many channels you can receive.

10 But how do cable companies pick up signals transmitted from these faraway stations? They don't do it with just cables and towers. They incorporate another technology that has become **intrinsic** to modern communication systems: satellites.

The Sky *Isn't* the Limit

11 Satellites are transmitting devices that **orbit** Earth. The satellites that transmit television programs are called communication satellites. (To learn more about satellites, read the GPS article in *World Works, Level F,* Lesson 7.)

12 Here's how cable companies use communication satellites. The television station sends signals via radio waves up to a satellite. The satellite bounces the signals back to Earth, where the cable company picks them up at receiving stations called head-ends. Because the satellites are high above Earth, there's a clear line of sight between the satellites and the senders and receivers on Earth. This allows cable companies to collect signals that might originate from thousands of miles away and deliver them to subscribers through their system of cables.

13 If cable television already uses satellites, how does satellite television fit into the picture? Let's find out.

brokers (brō′-kərz) people who arrange to sell things for other people or businesses
orbit (ôr′-bət) to travel in a circular path around a larger object

My WORKSPACE

Fiber-optic cables improve cable television reception. Made from ultrathin threads of glass or plastic, these cables use light to transmit audio and video signals. **Think about how new technologies keep making television better.**

Summarize

Not all information in the text is important enough to be included in a summary. Reread **paragraph 12.** Write one detail you would **not** include in a summary of this paragraph.

____

____

Now look for the important ideas and use them to write a summary of the paragraph.

____

____

____

____

____

My WORKSPACE

Summarize

Sometimes you may need to summarize text that is several paragraphs long. Review the "Then Came DBS" section. Write down the **three** most important ideas in this section.

1. ______________________

____

2. ______________________

____

3. ______________________

____

Now use these three ideas to write a summary of the section. Remember that your summary should be about 20 words or less.

____

____

____

____

____

____

Then Came DBS

14 Have you seen the little dish-shaped structures attached to the sides of homes? These dishes are **concave** antennas that receive satellite signals for direct broadcast satellite (DBS) television. Much like the roof antennas used to pick up broadcast television signals, satellite dishes pick up the signals and send them to television sets via a small cable between the dish and the set.

15 The DBS system is similar to the satellite-assisted cable system, except that after the satellite signals bounce back to Earth, they don't travel to customers' homes through a cable. Instead, DBS broadcast centers collect the signals and send them back up to the satellites so that they can bounce back toward Earth and go directly to their customers' satellite dishes.

16 Maybe you've noticed that satellite dishes all point in the same direction: south. That's because all communication satellites orbit Earth at the **equator,** which, from the northern hemisphere, is south.

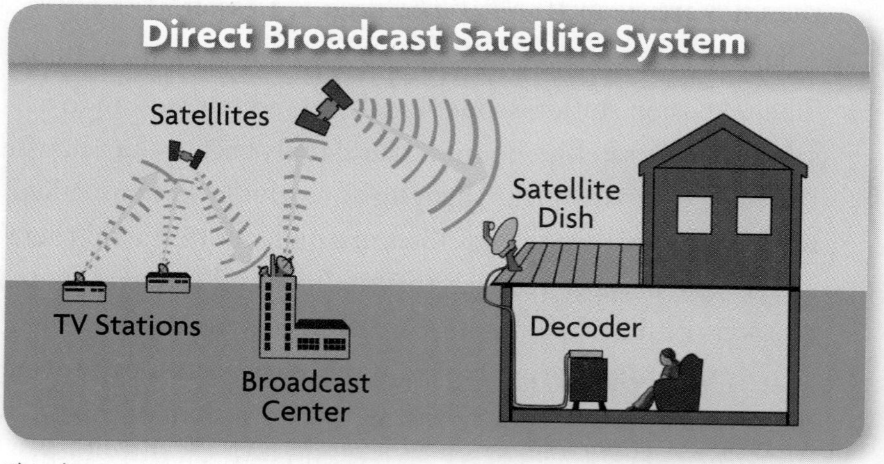

This diagram shows how DBS signals reach television sets. **Think about how DBS television allows people who live in remote or mountainous areas to receive television signals without needing cables.**

---

concave (kän-kāv′) curved inward, like the inside of a bowl

equator (i-kwā′-tər) an imaginary line that circles Earth halfway between the North and South Poles

Tricky Business

17 So why do satellite television users have to pay for television at all? Why can't they just pick up the program signals the first time the signals bounce back to Earth? Because people tried this a few decades ago, and the television stations protested.

18 Like cable television, the original idea for DBS television came from private citizens. In 1976, after the satellite-assisted cable television business was in full swing, an **ingenious** college professor built his own satellite dish to pick up the satellite signals that the cable companies were using. Other people quickly followed suit, buying satellite dishes and putting them in their backyards. Although these dishes, which were up to 12 feet (4 meters) in diameter, were very expensive, once they were purchased they allowed the viewer to receive signals from hundreds of stations for free.

19 The free ride ended, however, in 1984, after the broadcasters protested and Congress passed a law allowing all television broadcasters to encrypt, or encode, their satellite signals. This is why DBS viewers must have a small boxlike device connected to their television that decodes the signals for viewing. Cable viewers must use a similar device to view certain channels.

20 Satellite dish technology has come a long way since 1976. The dishes no longer need to be large and expensive. Today a personal satellite dish might be as small as 18 inches (46 cm) in diameter and cost only about $100.

21 All these television advances are good news for consumers because they allow people to choose the delivery system that best fits their individual needs.

Fun Facts

Many television stations offer recent episodes of certain shows on their Internet sites, so more and more computers are doubling as televisions.

My WORKSPACE

The top photo shows a large satellite dish much like the ones used in the 1970s. The bottom photo shows the smaller satellite dishes many people use today. **Think about how advances in technology often allow things to shrink in size yet work more efficiently.**

Self-Check

Look back at the prediction you wrote on page 28.

- Does your prediction match the text? Why or why not?

Write your answers on a separate sheet of paper.

A

Understanding What You Read

Fill in the circle next to the correct answer. You may look back at the text to help you choose the correct answers.

1. Which inference is **best** supported by the information in paragraph 5?

❍ A. If broadcast television had worked for everyone, cable television might never have been invented.

❍ B. If you live in a large city, chances are you won't be able to get broadcast television reception.

❍ C. Cable television works only for people who live in areas that can't get broadcast television.

2. The idea for cable television came from

❍ A. an ingenious college professor.

❍ B. brokers who wanted to make money.

❍ C. a community situated in a rural Pennsylvania valley.

3. Which of these types of television does **not** involve the use of satellites?

❍ A. broadcast television

❍ B. cable television

❍ C. DBS television

4. The diagram titled "Direct Broadcast Satellite System" helps support the author's point that

❍ A. all communication satellites orbit Earth at the equator.

❍ B. the idea for satellite television came from private citizens.

❍ C. there's a clear line of sight between satellites and receivers.

5. What caused Congress to pass a law in 1984 to protect broadcasters?

❍ A. Broadcasters were not able to provide enough program choices.

❍ B. People found a way to get cable television programs for free.

❍ C. Cable television companies decided to encrypt their signals.

Score 4 points for each correct answer.

________ /20 **Total Score: Activity A**

B

Summarizing

Paragraphs 8 and 9 from the article are shown below. Read the paragraphs. Then use the paragraphs to complete the activities.

Today more than 65 million U.S. homes have cable television. One thing that has boosted cable's popularity is the fact that cable companies can offer viewers a wide array of programs from stations all across the country—and even the world.

Most cable companies don't create the programs you watch. Instead, they operate as brokers. They negotiate contracts with the individual stations or networks that create the programs. The number of stations your cable company contracts with determines how many channels you can receive.

1. Fill in the circle next to a detail that is **not** important enough to include in a summary of these two paragraphs.

❍ A. More than 65 million U.S. homes have cable television.

❍ B. Cable companies can offer a wide array of programs from all across the country.

❍ C. The number of stations your cable company contracts with determines the number of channels you receive.

2. Complete the summary diagram below. Write the most important ideas from the paragraphs in the top boxes. Write your summary in the bottom box. Remember that your summary should be about 20 words or less.

Score 5 points each for numbers 1 and 2.

_______ /10 **Total Score: Activity B**

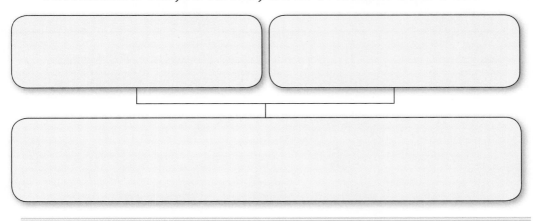

C

Using Words

Follow the instructions below. Write your answers on the lines.

1. List **three** things your teacher has **motivated** you to do.

____

____

____

2. List **two** details about where your school is **situated.**

____

____

3. List **two** things in nature that display an **array** of colors.

____

____

4. List **two** things that are **intrinsic** to cities.

____

____

5. List **two** things an **ingenious** person might do.

____

____

Score 4 points for each correct answer.

________ /20 **Total Score: Activity C**

D

Writing About It

Write a Magazine Article Suppose you are a technology reporter. Write an article about broadcast, cable, and satellite television. Finish the sentences below to write your article. Be sure your writing matches the information in the text. Use the checklist on page 119 to check your work.

Today you have many choices when it comes to television. If you choose broadcast television, you will receive signals from ______________________

____

____

Cable television is more reliable than broadcast television because __________

____

____

If you choose DBS television, ______________________________

____

____

Cable and DBS companies encode their television signals to ______________

____

____

____

____

Lesson 3 Add your scores from activities A, B, and C to get your total score.

______ **A** Understanding What You Read

______ **B** Summarizing

______ **C** Using Words

______ **Total Score**

Multiply your **Total Score x 2** ________

This is your percentage score.

Record your percentage score on the graph on page 121.

UNIT ONE
WRAP-UP

Compare and Contrast

You read three articles about technology in Unit One. Think about the topic of each article. Then choose **two** of the articles. Write the titles of the articles in the Venn diagram below. In the left and right circles, write the differences in how each topic affects people's lives. In the section where the two circles overlap, write the similarities in how they affect people's lives.

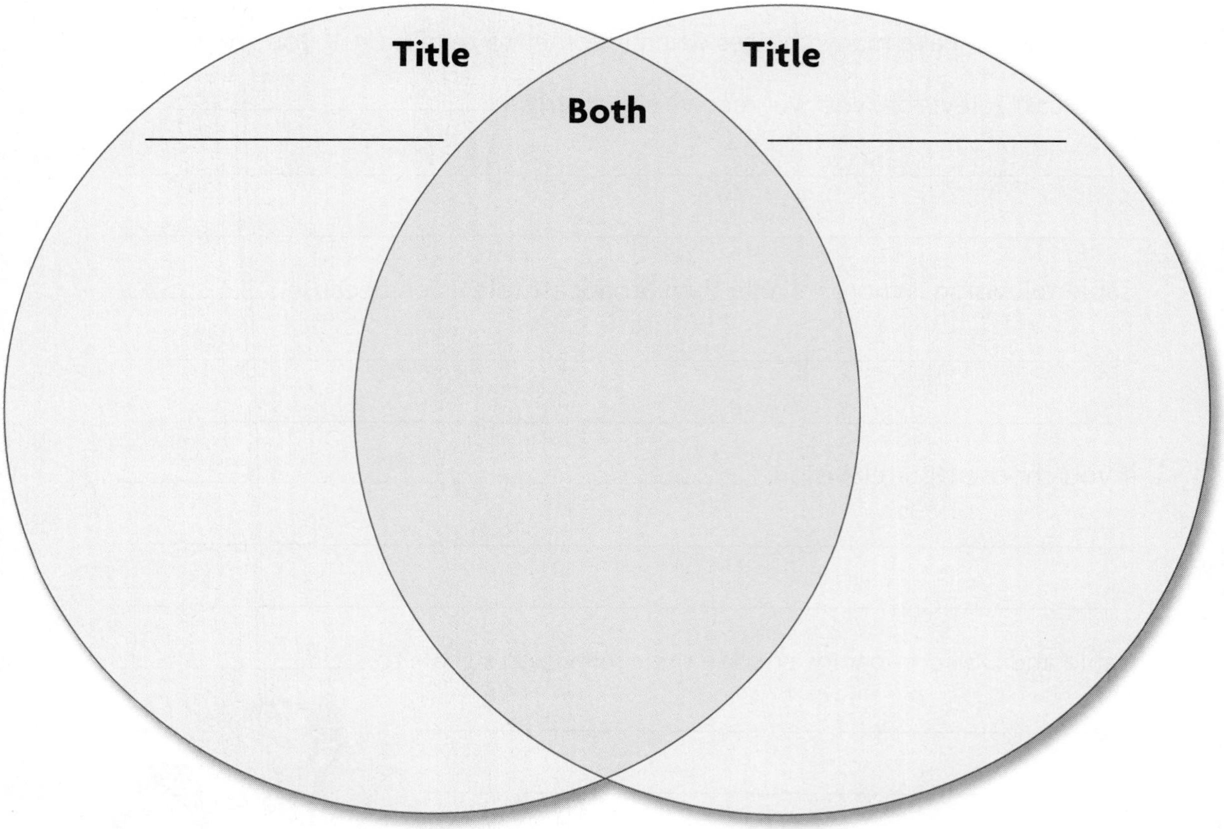

Use the diagram above to write a summary of how these technology topics are alike and different. Finish the sentences below to write your summary.

____________________ and ____________________ are different

because ____

____

____________________ and ____________________ are similar

because ____

____

Unit 2

Food

Food Preservation
Red Beans
Small Red Beans
Frijoles Rojos Pequeños
CHILI
NO BEANS
Organic
Apples
$2.99
PER POUND
Chocolate
Organic Food

Chocolate
Treat from a Tree

Chocolate has been a popular treat for centuries.

LESSON 4

READING SKILL

Making Connections

Good readers **make connections** to the text as they read. Strong connections include details that help you understand the text in a deeper or more personal way. There are three types of connections.

	connects text to . . .
Text-to-self ⟶	your own personal experiences.
Text-to-text ⟶	something you've read or seen on TV or film.
Text-to-world ⟶	events in the world or a story in the news.

EXAMPLE

Chocolate is popular because of its taste, but some experts believe the reason for chocolate's popularity goes beyond that. Chocolate has certain ingredients that trigger specific chemical reactions in a person's body. Many scientists point out that these chemical changes can produce feelings of excitement and happiness.

Look at these three possible connections to the example paragraph above.

Text-to-self When I read about how chocolate's taste makes it popular, it reminds me of my mom because she makes me delicious hot cocoa on cold days.

Text-to-text When I read about how chocolate causes reactions in the body, it reminds me of a book I read because it described how the body reacts to sugar.

Text-to-world When I read about how chocolate can affect people's feelings, it reminds me of a news story about what people eat because the reporter said that making healthy eating choices can have a positive effect on a person's emotions.

Complete the sentence below to make your own connection to the example paragraph. Then write what type of connection you made.

When I read about ____

it reminds me ____

____

because ____

____

What type of connection did you make? ____________________

Getting Ready to Read

Think About What You Know

CONNECT What are some kinds of chocolate treats? What do you know about how chocolate candy is made? Write your answers here.

___

___

___

Word Power

PREVIEW Read the words and definitions below. Then look ahead at the title and at the headings and images in the article.

maturity (mə-cho͞or′-ə-tē)	the state of being fully grown or developed
initiating (i-ni′-shē-āt′-ing)	starting something
modify (mä′-də-fī′)	to make minor changes to something
aroma (ə-rō′-mə)	a strong, pleasing smell
palatable (pa′-lə-tə-bəl)	having an agreeable taste

QUESTION Use the words, title, headings, and images to ask a question. What would you like to know about chocolate? Write your question on the lines below.

___

___

___

Reason to Read

Read to find out if the information in the text answers your question. At the end of the article, you will be asked to look back at your question. You will decide whether or not your question is answered in the text.

Chocolate
Treat from a Tree

1 It was once so valuable that the Aztec people used it to pay taxes. When Spanish and Portuguese explorers brought it back with them to Europe, they jealously guarded it from the rest of the continent for many years. Even after people in other countries learned about it, at first only the rich could afford it.

2 You might think we're talking about gold or a certain jewel, but it's actually something that you can get in cookies, ice cream, and the checkout lane at the supermarket. We're talking, of course, about the mouthwatering treat known as chocolate.

From Trees to Treats

3 To become the delicious treat we love, chocolate goes through many steps, starting with a simple bean. The bean is produced by cacao trees, which are found in warm, rainy climates within 20 degrees of the **equator**; today most cacao plantations are in Africa, Central and South America, and Southeast Asia. Because the trees prefer shade, farmers give them protection from direct sunlight by planting them among tall, broadleaf trees such as banana trees and coconut palms.

4 The beans are contained in pods produced by the trees. The football-shaped pods, which vary in length from four inches (10 cm) to more than a foot (30 cm), start out green or yellow and usually turn orange or red as they ripen. It takes five or six months for pods to reach **maturity.** Harvests twice a year result in about 30 pods per tree per year. Inside each pod, the beans (an average of 40 per pod) are covered in a sticky white pulp.

equator (i-kwā′-tər) the imaginary line around the middle of Earth that is the same distance from the North Pole as it is from the South Pole

My WORKSPACE

Connect

Some readers tend to make mostly text-to-self connections. Good readers push themselves to make text-to-text and text-to-world connections as well. Use the information in **paragraphs 1** and **2** to try to make a text-to-text connection. Complete the sentence below.

When I read about how valuable chocolate was long ago, it reminds me

____

____

____

because ______________

____

____

What type of connection did you make?

____

My WORKSPACE

Connect

Use the information in **paragraph 6** to make a strong connection. Try to make a text-to-world connection. Complete the sentence below.

When I read about ______

______

______

it reminds me ______

______

______

because ______

______

______

What type of connection did you make?

______

5 But how do these beans get from the tree to the checkout lane at your supermarket? It involves a process that starts with lots of hard work on cacao plantations.

Down on the Farm

6 Because the trees would be easily damaged if machines were used to harvest the pods, the pods are harvested by hand. This is no easy task. Plantation workers cut the pods from the trees using hook-shaped blades attached to poles or long, sharp knives called machetes.

7 After they've been taken from the tree, the pods are split open—usually with machetes—and the pulp and beans are removed. The pulp-covered raw beans, which are tough and bitter and taste nothing like chocolate, are put in boxes or piles and covered with banana leaves for about a week. The pulp ferments, heating up to as high as 140°F (60°C) and **initiating** a chemical reaction that causes the internal structure of the beans to break down. Different substances in the beans then combine to **modify** the beans' flavor, bringing it a little closer to the chocolate taste you're familiar with.

Workers carefully harvest the pods with machetes or with blades attached to long poles. Because the work has to be done by hand, it requires a lot of hard labor from the plantation workers. **Think about why harvesting the pods this way is such challenging work.**

8 After fermentation, to prevent them from getting moldy, the beans are dried in the sun for several days. If there is too much rain, the beans might be kept inside and dried by machines that blow hot air on them. The dried beans are then put into large sacks and shipped to chocolate makers around the world.

The Chocolate Factory

9 Once the beans arrive at the chocolate factory, workers sort them by type (there are three main types of cacao bean) and country of origin. The beans are then inspected and cleaned to remove any wood fibers, unusable beans, and pebbles.

10 The beans are now ready for roasting. The development of a fine chocolate flavor depends on roasting the beans at temperatures between 250°F and 350°F (121°C and 177°C) for up to two hours. This roasting is done in large rotating drums that allow the beans to heat evenly. Proper roasting removes any remaining moisture from the beans and brings out their distinct flavor, color, and **aroma.**

11 The hard shell that covers cacao beans needs to be removed from the bean—*when* it's removed usually depends on what product is being made. If it's cocoa powder (which you would use to make hot cocoa), the shell is usually removed before roasting. Leaving the shell on, though, allows for greater development of flavor; this is done when the chocolate is being made into candy.

12 The shells are removed through a process called winnowing. Machines crack the shell open and fans blow away the shell fragments, leaving behind the insides, or nibs, of the beans.

My WORKSPACE

Connect

Use the information in **paragraph 8** to make a strong connection.

What type of connection did you make?

Inside the cacao pod, the beans sit in a sticky pulp. **Think about how different raw beans must taste from the way a store-bought chocolate bar tastes.**

My WORKSPACE

Visualize

Reread **paragraph 15.** Use the details in the text to imagine what happens in a chocolate factory.

Draw what you are visualizing below.

Now complete the sentences below to describe what your visualization helps you imagine you would hear and feel there.

I hear ______________________

____

I feel ______________________

____

The News on Nibs

13 Nibs contain a mixture of cocoa solids and cocoa butter, which is the natural fat of the cacao bean. Nibs can be turned into three different things: chocolate liquor, cocoa butter, and cocoa powder.

14 Steel discs grind the nibs until the nibs release their fat and become a thick paste called chocolate liquor. If it's left to harden, the paste becomes the unsweetened chocolate that is often used for baking.

15 To get cocoa butter or cocoa powder, the chocolate liquor is processed further to separate the cocoa butter from the cocoa solids. A **hydraulic press** squeezes the thick, yellow cocoa butter out of the liquor, and the butter drains through screens. Once the cocoa butter has been drained from the liquor, the remaining cocoa solids are crushed into cocoa powder, which is used in baking and for chocolate drinks.

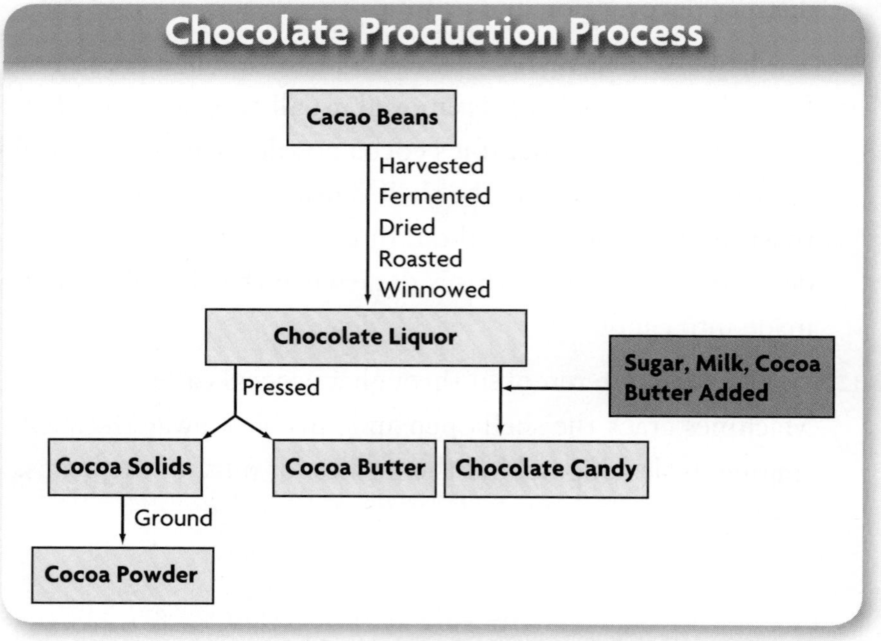

The chocolate production process varies depending on the type of product that is being made. **Think about what you would like to make if you had some cacao beans.**

hydraulic press (hī-drô′-lik-pres′) a machine that uses water to create a lot of pressure

A Matter of Taste

16 So what about that candy bar you can buy at the grocery store? Well, it's made by mixing some of the chocolate liquor with extra cocoa butter and a few other ingredients. For dark or semisweet chocolate, the chocolate liquor is combined with cocoa butter and sugar; if milk powder is added to the mixture, you get milk chocolate. White chocolate is made by mixing cocoa butter with sugar and milk powder—but it's not technically considered chocolate because it contains no chocolate liquor.

17 In any case, once the necessary ingredients are combined and moved through steel rollers, the mixture is conched, or continuously blended, ground, and stirred. This gives the chocolate a smooth texture. High-quality chocolate may be conched for several days. Next the chocolate is tempered, which involves raising and lowering the temperature to produce a smooth, glossy appearance. After that, the chocolate is molded into its final shape, wrapped, and shipped to a store near you.

18 As you can see, chocolate doesn't just fall from the tree and into the candy wrapper. A lot of hard work happens before it becomes not only **palatable** but delicious. So the next time you're nibbling on a candy bar or savoring a cup of cocoa, think about that humble little bean and the long, tough journey it has endured to put a smile on your face.

Did You Know?

What's in your chocolate? The gross fact is that a small amount of filth might have found its way into the chocolate you love. And this is no surprise to the U.S. government—they allow up to 60 insect fragments and one rodent hair in every 3.5 ounces (99 g) of chocolate!

My WORKSPACE

Think about the different shapes of the chocolate treats you've eaten.

Connect

Use the information in **paragraph 16** to make a strong connection.

What type of connection did you make?

Self-Check

Look back at the question you wrote on page 42.

- Does the information in the text answer your question? If it does, what is the answer? If it does not, where could you look to find more information?

Write your answers on a separate sheet of paper.

A

Understanding What You Read

Fill in the circle next to each correct answer. You may look back at the text to help you choose the correct answers.

1. Which inference is **best** supported by the information in the "From Trees to Treats" section?

- ❍ A. Cacao trees produce pods only in the summer.
- ❍ B. Cacao trees are taller than coconut palms.
- ❍ C. Cacao trees do not grow in the desert.

2. How does the pulp affect the raw cacao beans after they're covered with banana leaves?

- ❍ A. It gives them a smooth, shiny texture.
- ❍ B. It heats them, making them develop a more chocolatelike flavor.
- ❍ C. It prevents the growth of mold by removing any moisture remaining in them.

3. In the diagram titled "Chocolate Production Process," which of these steps has to happen **before** the beans are pressed?

- ❍ A. grinding
- ❍ B. fermenting
- ❍ C. adding milk

4. High-quality chocolate

- ❍ A. may be conched for several days.
- ❍ B. contains only cocoa butter and sugar.
- ❍ C. is made from the finest cocoa powder.

5. The information in the "Did You Know?" box on page 47 tells you

- ❍ A. important information about the big ideas in the article.
- ❍ B. what the author thinks about an issue in the article.
- ❍ C. a surprising fact about the topic of the article.

Score 4 points for each correct answer.

_______/20 **Total Score: Activity A**

B

Making Connections

Paragraph 3 from the article is shown below. Read the paragraph. Then use the paragraph to complete the activities.

To become the delicious treat we love, chocolate goes through many steps, starting with a simple bean. The bean is produced by cacao trees, which are found in warm, rainy climates within 20 degrees of the equator; today most cacao plantations are in Africa, Central and South America, and Southeast Asia. Because the trees prefer shade, farmers give them protection from direct sunlight by planting them among tall, broadleaf trees such as banana trees and coconut palms.

1. Complete the sentence below to make a connection to the paragraph above. Try to make your connection a text-to-text connection.

When I read about ______________________________

____

it reminds me ______________________________

____

because ______________________________

____

2. Complete the sentence below to make another connection to the paragraph above. Try to make this connection a text-to-world connection.

When I read about ______________________________

____

it reminds me ______________________________

____

because ______________________________

____

Score 5 points each for numbers 1 and 2.

________ /10 **Total Score: Activity B**

C

Using Words

Complete each sentence with a word from the box. Write the missing word on the line.

maturity	**initiating**	**modify**
aroma	**palatable**	

1. We smelled the wonderful ______________________ of freshly baked cookies when we entered the house.

2. The bread was so stale that it was no longer______________________.

3. When my sister and I discovered that the movie was sold out, we had to

______________________ our plans for the evening.

4. By the time my puppy grows to ______________________, she will have lost her puppy teeth and grown her adult teeth.

5. He often had a difficult time ______________________ conversations with people he did not know.

Choose one word from the box. Write a new sentence using the word. Be sure to put at least one detail in your sentence. The detail should show that you understand what the word means. Use the sentences above as examples.

6. ____

____

Score 4 points for each correct answer in numbers 1–5.
(Do not score number 6.)

________ /20 **Total Score: Activity C**

D

Writing About It

Write a Journal Entry Suppose your class went on a tour of a chocolate factory. Write a journal entry about this experience. Finish the sentences below to write your journal entry. Be sure your writing matches the information in the text. Use the checklist on page 119 to check your work.

Today our class took a tour of a chocolate factory. Our tour guide told us how chocolate is made. Chocolate begins as cacao beans, which grow

____

____

After the beans are taken from the trees and before they're sent to the factory, they are ____

____

At the factory, after the workers sort and clean the beans, they roast them by

____

____

We learned that the insides of the beans, called nibs, can be turned into three different things: ______________________________

____

Then we watched the factory workers turn chocolate liquor into

____

We tasted samples and they were delicious!

Lesson 4 Add your scores from activities A, B, and C to get your total score.

_______ **A** Understanding What You Read

_______ **B** Making Connections

_______ **C** Using Words

_______ **Total Score**

Multiply your **Total Score x 2** _________

This is your percentage score.

Record your percentage score on the graph on page 121.

Food Preservation
KEEPING GOOD FOOD GOOD

Refrigerators do more than keep your food cool and refreshing. They also help keep your food fresh and safe to eat.

READING SKILL Asking Questions

Good readers **ask questions** before, during, and after reading. Asking questions can help you set a purpose for reading. It can also help you stay interested in the text and find more meaning as you read. Sometimes your questions will be answered in the text. At other times you will have to find the answers on your own. You could do this by asking your teacher or another student for help. You could also look for the answer on the Internet or in a book or magazine at the library.

EXAMPLE

When packing a lunch for school, there are many decisions to be made. Should you bring a turkey sandwich or peanut butter and jelly? A piece of fruit or a cup of yogurt? The answers to these questions might depend on what kind of container you will use to carry your lunch. Food stays fresher longer in an insulated lunch box with an ice pack than it does in a paper bag.

Which container keeps food fresher longer, an insulated lunch box or a paper bag? is a good question to ask yourself as you read the example paragraph above. This question is answered in the last sentence of the paragraph.

What kinds of foods tend to spoil quickly? is another good question you might ask. This question is *not* answered in the paragraph text. To find the answer, you would need to use other sources that go beyond the text. On the lines below, write one thing you could do to find the answer.

____

____

Now think about the article you are about to read. Use the photo and caption on the previous page and what you already know to ask a question about food preservation. Write your question on the lines below.

____

____

Getting Ready to Read

Think About What You Know

CONNECT Think about the foods you like to eat. What do you know about how these foods are kept fresh and safe to eat? Write your answer here.

____

____

____

Word Power

PREVIEW Read the words and definitions below. Then look ahead at the title and at the headings and images in the article.

disadvantages (dis′-əd-van′-tij-əz)	conditions that cause problems or that make it hard to succeed
indefinitely (in-de′-fə-nət-lē)	for a period of time with no clear ending
deteriorates (di-tir′-ē-ə-rāts′)	becomes worse in condition
sterile (ster′-əl)	free from germs
altered (ôl′-tərd)	changed in some way

PREDICT Use the words, title, headings, and images to make a prediction. What do you think the author will say about food preservation?

I predict the author will ____

____

because ____

____

Reason to Read

Read to find out if the prediction you wrote above matches the information in the text. At the end of the article, you will be asked about your prediction. You will need to explain how your prediction is the same as the text or different from it.

Food Preservation
KEEPING GOOD FOOD GOOD

1 Suppose you're making a turkey sandwich with some mayonnaise for lunch. You also decide to throw in some dried fruit and a glass of milk.

2 Sounds like a simple enough lunch, right? But imagine if you had to roast the turkey that morning while gathering eggs for the mayonnaise, milking the cow, and picking the fruit! Luckily, there are food preservation techniques that help us keep food fresh longer so we don't have to use it immediately.

When Good Food Goes Bad

3 Food begins spoiling immediately after it's removed from its life source—that is, meat begins to decay when an animal is slaughtered, and fruits and vegetables begin to rot as soon as they're harvested. This decay is caused by bacteria that exist in the food or that settle on the food from the surrounding air. Because bacteria thrive in warm, moist conditions, allowing food to sit exposed at room temperature makes it a prime target for bacterial growth.

4 The taste and texture of spoiled food is disgusting, as you know if you have ever accidentally swallowed sour milk or taken a bite of rotten fruit. But the more serious concern is that consuming high levels of the bacteria found in spoiled food can make you sick.

5 Even before humans were aware of bacteria, they knew that rotting food causes sickness. But eating only fresh foods wasn't practical due to the huge size of many meat animals and the fact that fruits and vegetables don't grow in the cold winter months. So people had to find ways to make their food last longer without allowing bacteria to take over. Storing meat in cold caves, covering fish with salt, and drying fruit in the sun were a few of the ancient techniques used to preserve food.

My WORKSPACE

Visualize

Use the details in the shaded text to visualize how people preserved food long ago.

Draw a picture of what you are visualizing in the box below.

How does your visualization help you better understand the text?

___

___

___

My WORKSPACE

Canning food can keep it safe to eat for years. **Think about what kinds of canned foods you eat.**

Ask Questions

Reread **paragraph 9.** What question would you like to ask about the information in this paragraph? Write your question on the lines below.

____

____

____

How does asking this question help you find more meaning as you read?

____

____

____

____

6 Today we use very similar methods as well as several more advanced techniques. The most effective techniques involve changing a food's temperature, controlling moisture, adding chemicals, or exposing food to radiation. As you will see, each approach has its benefits and **disadvantages.**

Chill Out

7 You're probably familiar with one of the most common devices used in modern food preservation. It's big, it hums, and it's found in the kitchen: it's the refrigerator!

8 Because bacteria grow more slowly in cold temperatures, refrigeration extends the time that food stays fresh. Refrigerators keep air temperature between 32°F and 40°F (0°C and 4°C), greatly slowing down bacterial growth. And while some foods last only about a week in the refrigerator, the taste and texture of most refrigerated foods are not affected for many days.

9 Putting food in the freezer extends the life of the food even further. When the food is stored at 32°F or below, bacterial growth halts completely, which keeps food safe to eat **indefinitely.** But what about the recommended freezing times you see stamped on some frozen foods? These refer to the time before the food's quality—not its safety—**deteriorates.** While the food remains secure from bacterial growth, it doesn't maintain its quality forever. Too much time in the freezer can dry out the food, resulting in an unpleasant effect on its color, texture, and taste.

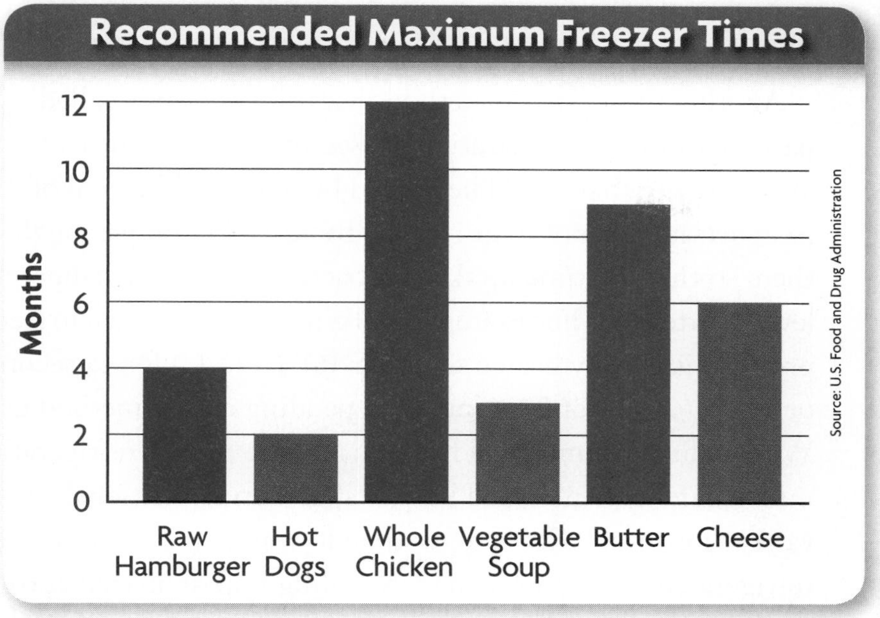

This bar graph shows the recommended times for storing certain foods in the freezer. Remember, they will still be safe to eat after the recommended time period, but they will not taste as good. **Think about what food tastes like when it has been in the freezer too long.**

Can't Take the Heat

10 While cold slows down or stops bacterial growth, high heat kills bacteria outright. This makes boiling food—the principle behind canned foods—an effective method of food preservation. After a can is filled with peas, for example, it's **vacuum-sealed.** This prevents any more bacteria from entering it. Then the can is boiled to kill the bacteria already inside it. The peas inside the can remain **sterile** until the can is opened, at which point bacteria in the air begin to attack the food. This is why you see the words *Refrigerate After Opening* on canned and bottled goods.

11 As with other methods of food preservation, taste and texture are **altered** during this process. Canned food can be stored for years and still be safe to eat, but its shelf life is not infinite because some chemical changes still occur within the sealed can. You should always look for a *Best Before* or *Use By* date on a can to make sure the food's quality is still at its best.

vacuum-sealed (va'-kūm-sēld') closed with an airtight seal

My WORKSPACE

Ask Questions

Reread **paragraph 10.** What question would you like to ask about the information in this paragraph? Write your question on the lines below.

____

____

____

How does asking this question help you stay engaged with the text as you read?

____

____

____

____

My WORKSPACE

Ask Questions

Reread **paragraph 12.** What question would you like to ask about the information in this paragraph? Write your question on the lines below.

____

____

____

How does asking this question help you stay interested in the text?

____

____

____

____

The government requires irradiated food to carry this symbol on its packaging. This helps shoppers make their food choices, because some people question whether irradiated food is healthy and might not want to buy it. **Think about why there might be concern about whether irradiated foods are healthy.**

12 Another preservation method that utilizes heat is called pasteurization. Pasteurization is used on products with a taste and a texture that would be ruined by boiling. The goal of pasteurization is not to kill *all* the bacteria, but only enough of them so that the time it takes for bacteria to reach a dangerous level is extended. For example, milk, a commonly pasteurized product, is usually heated to either 161°F (72°C) for 15 seconds or 145°F (63°C) for 30 minutes, depending on the method used. With reduced numbers of bacteria and the proper refrigeration, milk is safe to drink—and keeps its taste and nutritional value—for several days longer than it would be if the milk were refrigerated but left untreated. Standing unpasteurized at room temperature, the milk would last for just hours instead of days.

13 But food preservation isn't just a hot-and-cold issue. Let's take a look at the moisture factor.

Dry It Out

14 Without water, bacteria can't grow and reproduce. This means that dehydrating, or removing moisture from, food is another way to slow bacterial growth and reduce spoilage. The result is a shriveled, toughened version of the original—think of the small, dried raisin that comes from a plump, juicy grape.

15 Dehydration can be accomplished with common kitchen ingredients such as salt and sugar. For example, a cup of salt poured on two pounds of fish or a cup of sugar mixed into a pound of fruit eventually absorbs the moisture from the food. Hot and cold temperatures can dry foods as well. Blasting food with hot air (to make banana chips, for example) or laying it out in the sun (to get sun-dried tomatoes or raisins) evaporates the food's moisture. And freeze-drying food eliminates moisture as the food freezes.

Food Preservation Thermometer

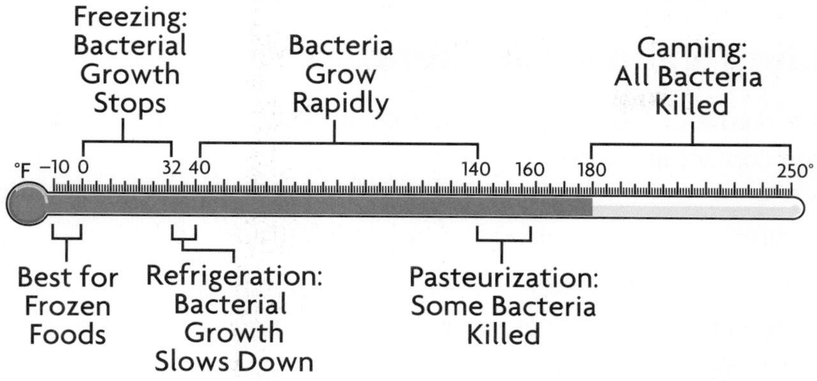

Source: National Center for Home Food Preservation

This graphic shows how the temperatures of different food preservation techniques affect bacteria. **Think about what foods are commonly preserved within the different temperature ranges shown above.**

Other Methods

16 Maybe you've seen some unusual words among the ingredients on food labels. These are probably the names of preservatives, which are chemicals put into food to slow bacterial growth. These chemicals make foods such as cereals, snack bars, and lunch meats last longer. There is concern that some preservatives may adversely affect health, but most are considered safe.

17 One relatively new food preservation method is irradiation. Food is briefly exposed to energy such as **X-rays.** The energy damages bacterial cells in such a way that when the bacteria try to reproduce, they die instead. Red meat, **poultry,** and some fruits and vegetables are the most frequently irradiated foods.

18 So the next time you take some vegetables from the freezer, open a can of soup, or chew on some dried fruit, think about what kept that food edible. And realize that, while it might not taste the same as it does when it's fresh, we should feel lucky that we have food preservation techniques to keep that food safe to eat for so long.

X-rays (eks′-rāz′) beams of a type of energy that can go through solid objects; often used to take pictures of the inside of the body

poultry (pōl′-trē) meat from chickens, ducks, or turkeys

My WORKSPACE

Ask Questions

Reread the questions you wrote on pages 56, 57, and 58.

Which questions are answered in the text? Write the answers on a separate sheet of paper.

Did you ask any questions that are *not* answered in the text? If so, where could you look to find the information that would answer each question? Write the answers on a separate sheet of paper.

Self-Check

Look back at the question you wrote on page 53.

- Does the information in the text answer your question? If it does, what is the answer? If it does not, where could you look to find more information?

Now look back at the prediction you wrote on page 54.

- Does your prediction match the text? Why or why not?

Write your answers on a separate sheet of paper.

A

Understanding What You Read

Fill in the circle next to the correct answer. You may look back at the text to help you choose the correct answers.

1. Freezing food is different from canning food because freezing food

❍ A. kills most, but not all, bacteria.

❍ B. stops bacteria from growing but does not kill them.

❍ C. damages bacterial cells so that they die if they try to reproduce.

2. Pasteurization is used on products with a taste and a texture that would be ruined by

❍ A. boiling.

❍ B. stirring.

❍ C. freezing.

3. What is the effect of laying tomatoes out in the sun?

❍ A. The tomatoes produce salt and sugar to fight bacterial growth.

❍ B. Bacteria can't reproduce because the moisture is removed.

❍ C. X-rays destroy any bacteria inside the food.

4. The diagram titled "Food Preservation Thermometer" helps support the author's point that

❍ A. warm conditions are best for bacterial growth.

❍ B. without water, bacteria cannot grow and reproduce.

❍ C. too much time in the freezer can affect a food's taste.

5. From what the author told you about different food preservation techniques, you can conclude that

❍ A. a cold cave is the safest place to store meat.

❍ B. people should boil their food before they eat it.

❍ C. if your power goes out, it's safe to eat canned food.

Score 4 points for each correct answer.

________/20 **Total Score: Activity A**

B Asking Questions

Paragraph 3 from the article is shown below. Read the paragraph. Then use the paragraph to complete the activities.

Food begins spoiling immediately after it's removed from its life source—that is, meat begins to decay when an animal is slaughtered, and fruits and vegetables begin to rot as soon as they're harvested. This decay is caused by bacteria that exist in the food or that settle on the food from the surrounding air. Because bacteria thrive in warm, moist conditions, allowing food to sit exposed at room temperature makes it a prime target for bacterial growth.

1. Read each question below. Then fill in the circle next to the question that is answered in the paragraph above.

- ❍ A. What kinds of bacteria are usually found in food?
- ❍ B. What types of animals are slaughtered for food?
- ❍ C. What causes meat, fruits, and vegetables to rot?

2. Write a new question about the paragraph above. The answer to this question should *not* be given in the paragraph text. Then write **two** ways you could find the answer on your own.

Question ______________________________

____

Two Ways I Could Find the Answer

1. ______________________________

____

2. ______________________________

____

Score 5 points each for numbers 1 and 2.

________ /10 **Total Score: Activity B**

C

Using Words

The words and phrases in the list below relate to the words in the box. Some words or phrases in the list are synonyms. They have the same meaning. Some words or phrases are antonyms. They have the opposite meaning. Write the related word from the box on each line. Use each word from the box **twice.**

disadvantages	**indefinitely**	**deteriorates**
sterile	**altered**	

Synonyms

1. without end ______________________
2. revised ______________________
3. weaknesses ______________________
4. extremely clean ______________________
5. breaks down ______________________

Antonyms

6. improves ______________________
7. filthy ______________________
8. benefits ______________________
9. stayed the same ______________________
10. for a set amount of days ______________________

Score 2 points for each correct answer.

________ /20 **Total Score: Activity C**

D

Writing About It

Write a Poster Suppose you are asked to make a poster that shows some of the ways common household foods are preserved. Finish the sentences below to write your poster. Be sure your writing matches the information in the text. Use the checklist on page 119 to check your work.

Popular Ways to Preserve Food

Keeping Food Safe

- Freezing food such as vegetables helps preserve the food by ______________________

  ____

  ____

- Canning food such as chicken soup helps preserve the food by ______________________

  ____

  ____

- Pasteurizing food such as milk helps preserve the food by______________________

  ____

  ____

Lesson 5 Add your scores from activities A, B, and C to get your total score.

_______ **A** Understanding What You Read

_______ **B** Asking Questions

_______ **C** Using Words

_______ **Total Score**

Multiply your **Total Score x 2** _________

This is your percentage score.

Record your percentage score on the graph on page 121.

Organic Food
Nature's Way

Organic apples look just like regular apples. The difference is in how they're grown.

READING SKILL Making Inferences

The text that authors write can have meanings on different levels. You can understand the text on one level by simply reading and thinking about each word. But when you also use use your own ideas and experiences to think about the text, you are **making inferences.** Good readers combine the information in the text with their own knowledge to make inferences.

For example, think about the sentence *The ice cream melted very quickly.* You can read this sentence to mean simply that it didn't take long for the ice cream to melt. However, if you are making an inference, you can read the sentence to mean "It must be a hot day, because the ice cream didn't last long before it melted."

EXAMPLE

MaryJane Butters has been an organic farmer in Idaho for more than 20 years. Her farm was one of the first certified organic farms in the state. About the organic label on her crops, Butters says she prefers no label at all. "I want to call my organic carrots 'carrots' and let other farmers call theirs a 'chemical carrot,'" she says in an interview on her Web site.

An inference can be big or small. A small inference is one that is very close in meaning to the original text. The meaning of a big inference is much broader.

Small Inference
MaryJane Butters has years of experience as an organic farmer.

Big Inference
Organic farmers don't use chemicals to grow their crops.

Notice that the words and meaning in the small inference are similar to the original text. The idea in the big inference, however, is broader. It applies to how organic farmers grow their crops and not just to MaryJane Butters and her farm.

Use the information in the text and what you already know to make another inference. Then explain why it's a small or big inference.

____

____

This is a ____________ inference because ____________

____

Getting Ready to Read

Think About What You Know

CONNECT What kinds of food have you seen labeled with the word *organic*? What do you know about organic food? Write your answers here.

____

____

____

Word Power

PREVIEW Read the words and definitions below. Then look ahead at the title and at the headings and images in the article.

synthetic (sin-the′-tik)	composed of human-made substances instead of being found in nature
conventional (kən-vench′-nəl)	following accepted standards or customs
assert (ə-sərt′)	to state strongly and positively
sanitary (sa′-nə-ter′-ē)	free of dirt and germs that can be harmful to health
comparable (käm′-prə-bəl)	alike enough to be compared

QUESTION Use the words, title, headings, and images to ask a question. What would you like to know about organic food? Write your question on the lines below.

____

____

____

Reason to Read

Read to find out if the information in the text answers your question. At the end of the article, you will be asked to look back at your question. You will decide whether or not your question is answered in the text.

Organic Food
Nature's Way

1 Imagine finding two kinds of apples at the store. Although one is more expensive, they look and feel alike, making it impossible to detect any difference. A sign in the store describes the more expensive apple as "organic." But what exactly does this mean?

Harm on the Farm?

2 Organic food is defined not by how it looks, feels, or even tastes, but in how it's grown or raised. Food labeled with the word *organic* is grown by farmers who promote the protection of the environment, the use of **renewable resources,** and the health and well-being of animals and people.

3 Organic farming cropped up as a reaction against modern farming techniques. Though chemical fertilizers had been used since the 1800s, it was after World War II that most farmers began relying on new technologies and **synthetic** chemicals to produce crops and raise livestock. Over time many farmers began to suspect that these chemicals could harm the environment and people's health, so they turned to organic farming.

4 To understand exactly what organic farming is, first we need to understand the methods used by **conventional** farmers. Let's start by looking at how these farmers grow crops.

Modern Crops

5 Generally, farmers do all they can to maximize crop production. They add fertilizer, a substance that helps plants grow, to the soil in which crops are produced. Conventional farmers use synthetic fertilizers made of chemicals or of sewage sludge from waste treatment facilities.

renewable resources (ri-no͞o′-ə-bəl-rē′-sôrs′-əz) energy sources that don't run out because nature quickly replaces them

Infer

Reread the shaded text. Use the information in the text to make a small inference about farming after World War II. Remember that a small inference is similar to the original text. Write your inference here.

____

____

____

____

My WORKSPACE

Infer

Reread the shaded text. Use the information in the text and what you already know to make an inference, big or small, about the meaning of the text. Write your inference here.

____

____

____

____

This is a ______________

inference because ______

____

____

____

Organic strawberry farmers bring in small animals called hedgehogs to eat slugs that harm the plants. **Think about why using natural predators to control pests is considered an organic farming method.**

6 Pests, such as insects, can do serious damage to crops. To keep pests away or even to kill them, conventional farmers spray plants with synthetic compounds called pesticides. They might also use **irradiation** on the harvested crops or grow genetically modified crops that are designed to be resistant to certain pests. (To learn more about these kinds of crops, read about genetically modified foods in *World Works, Level F*, Lesson 3.) And to kill weeds that choke crops and steal nutrients from the soil, conventional farmers spray synthetic products called herbicides on their fields.

7 Many experts argue that using these chemicals not only adversely affects the soil, but that it also could pollute and poison a community's water supply. In addition, there is concern that killing off large populations of insects and weeds upsets the balance of nature.

8 And people's health is a concern as well. Some experts worry that the harvested food might contain some of the chemicals. Although there is no definite evidence about this, consuming these chemicals could cause serious problems for people.

The Organic Answer

9 Organic farmers seek to break this dependence on chemicals. They **assert** that almost identical results can be achieved without using synthetic fertilizers, pesticides, and herbicides.

10 Much of the fertilizer used by organic farmers is made of decaying plant matter and animal manure. This lets farmers make use of renewable materials and avoid the use of chemicals. And unlike synthetic fertilizers, natural fertilizers actually make the soil healthier. For example, they increase the soil's ability to hold water, which helps prevent the erosion of the soil.

---

irradiation (i-rā′-dē-ā′-shən) a method of preserving food by exposing it to an invisible form of energy that causes bacteria to die

11 To combat pests, organic farmers utilize a variety of methods—none of which involve chemicals, irradiation, or genetically modified crops. For example, organic farmers might put netting on peach trees to keep squirrels out and aluminum foil around the base of plants to keep whiteflies away.

12 Organic farmers rely on natural methods of weed control, often just pulling out weeds by hand. They also spread mulch, a layer of material such as straw that discourages weed growth.

13 But crop production is only one part of farming. Organic farmers also raise livestock for meat and dairy products in different ways than conventional farmers do.

Animal Products

14 To maximize the output they get from their animals, conventional farmers often implant or inject growth **hormones** into the animals. These hormones make the animals grow faster and fatter and, as in the case of a cow, produce more milk. Conventional farmers often put **antibiotics** into their livestock's feed to protect the animals from diseases. And to make the most use of space, animals are sometimes kept in crowded pens or cages—living conditions that are not comfortable or **sanitary.**

Think about why organic farmers disapprove of packing animals into cages.

hormones (hôr′-mōnz′) chemicals made by the body that trigger certain responses in it

antibiotics (an′-tī′-bī-ä′-tiks) medicines designed to destroy harmful bacteria in the body

My WORKSPACE

Visualize

Reread the shaded text. Use the details in the text to visualize what the author is describing. Draw what you are visualizing below.

What do you already know that helped you visualize this? Write your answer below.

My WORKSPACE

To be able to use the USDA organic seal, farmers need to stick to organic methods. **Think about why the USDA keeps close track of who uses the label.**

Infer

Reread **paragraph 16.** Use the information in the text and what you already know to make an inference, big or small, about the meaning of the text. Write your inference here.

____

____

____

____

This is a ______________

inference because ______

____

____

____

15 Because organic farmers question whether these chemicals might harm people's health, they avoid giving animals growth hormones and let them grow naturally. And by giving animals sanitary housing and a balanced diet of organic feed, organic farmers believe they do not need to give animals antibiotics.

16 Organic farmers are also concerned about the treatment of animals. Crowded pens and cages cause the animals to feel stress, which can harm their health. To provide a better quality of life for the animals, organic farmers allow them to roam outdoors, giving cows and sheep access to pastures and chickens access to yards.

Truth in Advertising

17 At the store, you have probably seen stickers or labels on a piece of fruit, a package of meat, or a box of cereal stating that the product is organic. Foods can't be labeled organic unless they meet the standards of the **U.S. Department of Agriculture** (USDA).

18 The USDA strictly monitors organic farmers to make sure they're following the standards that qualify their food for the organic label. And if a manufacturer wants to claim organic status for a product, such as a jar of spaghetti sauce, it must make sure the product contains at least 95 percent organically produced ingredients. Otherwise the product cannot display the USDA organic logo.

Everything Has a Price

19 Organic products come with a price; namely, the price you pay at the register. The cost of organic items tends to be greater than **comparable** nonorganic items. The explanation for this is simple: it costs more to produce organic foods.

U.S. Department of Agriculture (ū′-es-di-pärt′-mənt-əv-a′-gri-kəl′-chər) the branch of the U.S. government that oversees food production and enforces laws regarding it

Organic Farms in the United States

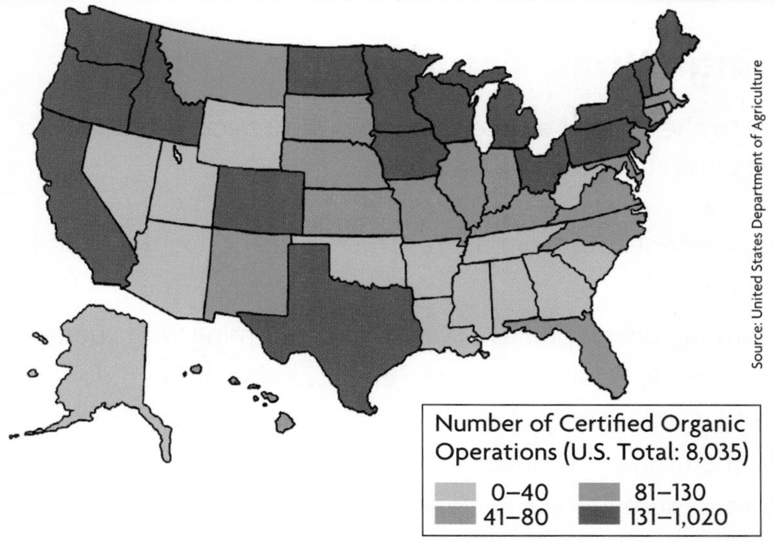

This map shows where most of the organic farms are in the United States. **Think about why some areas of the country have more organic farms than others.**

20 One reason for this is that organic foods require more labor. For example, it requires more time and people to pull weeds than to spray a field with herbicides. Another reason is that organic methods for insect and disease control are not always as effective as conventional methods. This means organic farmers run a higher risk of having their crops not grow and their livestock die.

21 Organic food continues to be a controversial subject. Many people point out that there is no scientific evidence that the use of synthetic chemicals in farming harms people's health. Others believe that it's only a matter of time before we see harmful effects. People also argue about how much damage conventional farming really does to animals and to the environment.

22 But the decisions aren't up to only the farmers and other experts. Today there are more organic farms in the United States than ever before, especially in California and in some upper Midwest states. And more stores carry both conventional and organic products. Because you—the consumer—can choose what to buy, there's a lot to take into consideration when you shop for something as simple as an apple.

My WORKSPACE

Self-Check

Look back at the question you wrote on page 66.

- Does the information in the text answer your question? If it does, what is the answer? If it does not, where could you look to find more information?

Write your answers on a separate sheet of paper.

A

Understanding What You Read

Fill in the circle next to the correct answer. You may look back at the text to help you choose the correct answers.

1. Which of these statements **best** summarizes the information in the "Harm on the Farm?" section?

- ❍ A. Organic farming developed as a way to avoid farming with chemicals that many considered harmful to the environment and people.
- ❍ B. After World War II, farmers began relying on new technologies that used chemicals to produce crops and raise livestock.
- ❍ C. One way to fix some of the damage that has been done to the environment is to use organic farming techniques.

2. Much of the fertilizer used by organic farmers is made of

- ❍ A. sludge from waste treatment plants.
- ❍ B. decaying plant matter and animal manure.
- ❍ C. mulch, which is a layer of material such as straw.

3. The caption for the photo on page 68 helps support the author's point that

- ❍ A. organic farmers find ways to fight pests that don't involve chemicals.
- ❍ B. killing large numbers of insects might upset the balance of nature.
- ❍ C. the use of natural fertilizers makes the soil healthier.

4. If you could rename the "Truth in Advertising" section, which of these would be the **best** choice?

- ❍ A. Shopping for Organic Food
- ❍ B. How Foods Earn the Organic Label
- ❍ C. The USDA's Beliefs on Organic Products

5. The map titled "Organic Farms in the United States" helps support the author's point that

- ❍ A. Organic farming can be very expensive.
- ❍ B. The number of organic farms is growing.
- ❍ C. There are many organic farms in California.

Score 4 points for each correct answer.

_________/20 **Total Score: Activity A**

B

Making Inferences

Paragraph 21 from the article is shown below. Read the paragraph. Then use the paragraph to complete the activities.

Organic food continues to be a controversial subject. Many people point out that there is no scientific evidence that the use of synthetic chemicals in farming harms people's health. Others believe that it's only a matter of time before we see harmful effects. People also argue about how much damage conventional farming really does to animals and to the environment.

1. Fill in the circle next to an inference that can be made from this paragraph.

❍ A. Not everyone is convinced that organic farming methods are necessary.

❍ B. People do not care if conventional farming harms animals and the environment.

❍ C. Most farmers agree that using a combination of farming techniques is the best way to do their work.

2. Use the information in the text and what you already know to make another inference. Write your inference on the lines below. Then explain why it's a small or big inference.

____

____

____

This is a ____________________ inference because ____________________

____

____

Score 5 points each for numbers 1 and 2.

________ /10 **Total Score: Activity B**

C

Using Words

Follow the instructions below. Write your answers on the lines.

1. List **two** things that are made of **synthetic** materials.

____

____

2. List **two** examples of **conventional** greetings.

____

____

3. List **two** beliefs that people might **assert.**

____

____

4. List **three** places that are usually kept **sanitary.**

____

____

____

5. List **two** pairs of things that are **comparable.**

____

____

Score 4 points for each correct answer.

________ /20 **Total Score: Activity C**

D

Writing About It

Write a Speech Suppose you are asked to give a speech about organic food. Write a speech that describes both the positive and the negative points about organic food. Finish the sentences below to write your speech. Be sure your writing matches the information in the text. Use the checklist on page 119 to check your work.

Food is considered organic when it ______________________________

____

____

An example of an organic farming method is ______________________

____

____

Organic farmers believe that conventional farming ________________

____

____

But organic food has problems too, such as ______________________

____

____

One of the main reasons people cannot agree on

whether organic farming is necessary is ______________

____

____

Lesson 6 Add your scores from activities A, B, and C to get your total score.

______ **A** Understanding What You Read

______ **B** Making Inferences

______ **C** Using Words

______ **Total Score**

Multiply your **Total Score x 2** ________

This is your percentage score.

Record your percentage score on the graph on page 121.

Compare and Contrast

You read three articles about food in Unit Two. Think about the topic of each article. Then choose **two** of the articles. Write the titles of the articles in the chart below. In the left and right columns, write the differences between the ways these topics affect people's lives. In the center column, write the similarities in the ways they affect people's lives.

Title ______	Similarities	Title ______

Use the chart above to write a summary of how these food topics are alike and different. Finish the sentences below to write your summary.

______ and ______ are different because ______

______

______ and ______ are similar because ______

______

Unit 3

Nature

Tsunamis
Force of Nature

The powerful waves of a tsunami (soo-nä′-mē) can destroy entire communities. These photos show an aerial view of Aceh Province, Indonesia, before and after the 2004 tsunami.

READING SKILL Reviewing the Reading Skills

You practiced three reading skills in Unit One. Rate your understanding of each skill using the chart below. Use the following rating scale:

3 I understand this skill well. I use it easily and correctly while I read.

2 I understand this skill a little bit. I sometimes use it correctly while I read.

1 I don't understand this skill. I am not able to use it while I read.

Mark the box under the number 3, 2, or 1 for each skill.

	3	2	1	Need to review?		Turn to:
Visualizing				Yes	No	Lesson 1, page 3
Finding the Main Idea and Details				Yes	No	Lesson 2, page 15
Summarizing				Yes	No	Lesson 3, page 27

If you rated your understanding of a skill at 2 or 1, look back at the lesson page where that skill was taught. The lesson page is shown in the chart above. Reread the skill definition and the example. This will help you get ready to complete the next lesson.

After you have reviewed the skills, complete the sentences below.

The skill I find most helpful when reading is ______________________________

because ____

____

During this lesson, one thing I can do to improve my reading is ______________

____

____

Getting Ready to Read

Think About What You Know

CONNECT When you hear the word *tsunami,* what does it remind you of? Why? What do you know about tsunamis and why they occur? Write your answers here.

____

____

____

Word Power

PREVIEW Read the words and definitions below. Then look ahead at the title and at the headings and images in the article.

misconception (mis′-kən-sep′-shən)	a false or mistaken idea
displaces (dis-plās′-əz)	moves something from its usual place or position
instantaneous (in′-stən-tā′-nē-əs)	occurring immediately
intensify (in-ten′-sə-fī′)	to make something greater or stronger
notorious (nō-tôr′-ē-əs)	well known for a bad or unpleasant reason

PREDICT Use the words, title, headings, and images to make a prediction. What do you think the author will say about tsunamis?

I predict the author will ______________________________

____

because ______________________________________

____

Reason to Read

Read to find out if the prediction you wrote above matches the information in the text. At the end of the article, you will be asked about your prediction. You will need to explain how your prediction is the same as the text or different from it.

Tsunamis
Force of Nature

1 On December 26, 2004, a massive earthquake occurred under the Indian Ocean. It triggered a tsunami, or series of giant waves, that killed nearly 300,000 people in more than 10 different countries in South Asia and East Africa. How did this happen?

What Causes a Tsunami?

2 First, let's clear up one popular **misconception** about tsunamis. Tsunamis are sometimes referred to as tidal waves—but tsunamis have nothing to do with **tides.** Rather, the deadly waves of a tsunami are created by a large-scale movement of earth that suddenly **displaces** a massive amount of water.

3 Tsunamis can be triggered by **landslides** that occur underwater or at the shoreline or, very rarely, by volcanic eruptions. But about 85 percent of tsunamis are caused by underwater earthquakes, so let's plunge right into the basics of why earthquakes occur.

The ABCs of Earthquakes

4 Earth's crust is composed of massive individual slabs of rock called tectonic plates. Beneath these plates lies a thick layer of molten rock that moves freely, causing the plates to move also.

5 Usually the plates move very slowly—between less than half an inch and four inches (one and 10 cm) per year. In the places where the plates come together, sometimes one plate pushes up against another and gets stuck there. Pressure builds in this spot until it finally forces the plates apart in a sudden and violent movement called an earthquake.

---

tides (tīdz) the cyclic rising and falling of the ocean relative to the shore that is caused by the pull of gravity from the moon and the sun
landslides (land′-slīdz′) sudden movements of large amounts of earth down a steep slope

My WORKSPACE

This photo, taken after a 1992 earthquake in California, shows what an upward shift in the earth's crust looks like. **Think about the amount of force it would take to create a shift of this size.**

Find the Main Idea

Reread **paragraph 5.** Determine whether the paragraph has a topic sentence or if you need to infer the main idea. Write the main idea below.

____

____

____

Explain how you determined your answer.

____

____

____

____

____

My WORKSPACE

Visualize

Reread the shaded text. Use the details in the text to imagine what happens in the water when someone does a "cannonball" jump into a pool. Draw what you are visualizing below.

What do you already know that helped you visualize this? Write your answer below.

6 A sufficiently violent earthquake beneath the sea can shift a large part of the sea floor upward very rapidly, and the shift might displace enough water to cause a tsunami. Think about what happens when you make a "cannonball" jump into a pool. Because you're curled into a ball as you enter the pool, your body displaces a large amount of water all at once. The water pushes out in all directions, causing waves.

7 The same sort of thing happens when the sea floor displaces water during an underwater earthquake. The only difference is the amount of water being moved. The 2004 earthquake that caused the deadly tsunami was one of the largest ever recorded. It caused the sea floor to rise several meters, which in turn caused an **instantaneous** displacement of more than seven cubic miles (30 cubic km) of water!

8 Now that we've discussed how tsunamis begin, let's see how the waves transform as they travel toward land.

Open Sea

9 Waves consist of high points, called crests, and low points, called troughs. In deep water, far out at sea, the waves aren't very tall. In fact, ships can pass over them without anyone aboard noticing anything unusual. That's because the push of the displaced water sends most of the tsunami's energy outward through the water, not upward toward the surface. The waves of the 2004 tsunami were only two feet (0.6 meter) high in deep water.

10 Although these deep-water waves are short in height, they are very long in length: the distance from crest to crest can be up to 60 miles (97 km). And the waves move with terrifying speed. Tsunamis can travel 500 miles (805 km) an hour, which is roughly the same speed as a commercial jet. This means a tsunami can cross the entire Pacific Ocean in less than a day.

11 As the tsunami nears shore and the ocean's depth decreases, the water has less room to move outward and begins to move upward instead. This causes the waves to increase in height, to slow down to about 30 miles (48 km) per hour, and to bunch closer together.

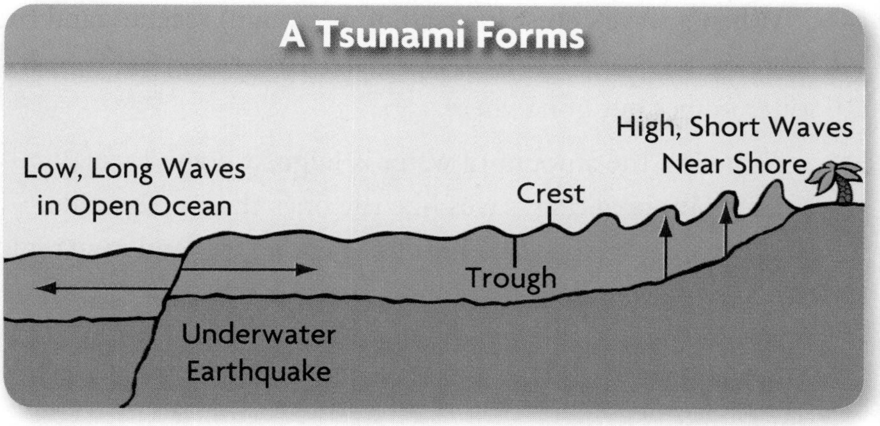

This diagram shows how the waves of a tsunami change as they approach the shore. **Think about how the distance between the earthquake and the shore might affect the size and power of the tsunami.**

The Wave Hits Land

12 The size of a tsunami when it hits land depends on the shape of the surrounding **geographical features.** For example, **coral reefs** can reduce the impact of a tsunami, but a particularly shallow bay can **intensify** it. That's why one community might be devastated while other communities nearby might experience little or no damage.

13 As a tsunami reaches the shore, often the trough of the wave arrives first. This causes a stunningly large drop in the water level at the shore—as much as several hundred feet—that can leave fish and other sea creatures flopping on the sand. Tragically, this phenomenon frequently attracts curious onlookers. They rush to the shore for the spectacle, only to become victims of the giant wave that inevitably hits seconds or minutes later and floods the land.

geographical features (jē′-ə-gra′-fi-kəl-fē′-cherz) features and formations of land, such as mountains and rivers

coral reefs (kôr′-əl-rēfs′) ridges of rocklike material formed by the gradual buildup of the skeletons of coral animals that grow in the ocean near the shoreline

My WORKSPACE

Visualize

Reread the shaded text. Use the details in the text to imagine what it looks like when the trough of the wave first reaches shore. Draw what you are visualizing in the box below.

Now write a description of what you are visualizing. Be sure to describe **at least two** parts of your visualization that are not described in the text. These parts come from your own experience and imagination.

My WORKSPACE

It can take weeks for the floodwaters from a tsunami to recede completely. This photo was taken in Sumatra, Indonesia, almost three weeks after the 2004 tsunami. **Think about what a town would need to do to recover after a tsunami.**

Summarize

Reread **paragraphs 17** and **18.** Write the **three** most important ideas in these paragraphs.

1. ____________________

____

2. ____________________

____

3. ____________________

____

Now use these three ideas to write a summary of the paragraphs.

____

____

____

____

____

14 When a wave's crest (instead of its trough) reaches land first, there are no warning signs—in an instant, the massive rush of water comes out of nowhere.

15 Although the amount of water is huge, it doesn't usually create giant breaking waves like the ones that surfers ride. Rather, the waves look similar to a very strong and very rapid rise in sea level. However, if breaking waves do form, they can be as high as 100 feet (30 meters). The waves of the 2004 tsunami that hit the land closest to the earthquake reached this height.

16 The volume of water in a tsunami wave wields so much force that it can wipe out entire coastal communities. Not only do the incoming waves destroy everything in their path, but many victims drown when the rush of water recedes and sweeps them out to sea. A second wave usually follows several minutes to an hour later, with additional waves arriving at similar intervals for two hours or more.

Warning Systems

17 No one can prevent tsunamis, but we can try to predict when they might occur. Because the Pacific Ocean is **notorious** for its frequent earthquakes, an international commission created a tsunami warning system that has its base of operations at the Pacific Tsunami Warning Center (PTWC) in Hawaii. At this center and at other regional centers, scientists receive data from devices that monitor earthquake activity along the ocean floor so that they can detect potential tsunamis and send out warnings as early as possible.

18 Because not all earthquakes result in tsunamis, and because evacuating people from homes and resorts is costly, a tsunami warning system must be accurate. So scientists have placed special wave gauges in the Pacific Ocean that can determine whether or not a tsunami is forming.

The Ring of Fire

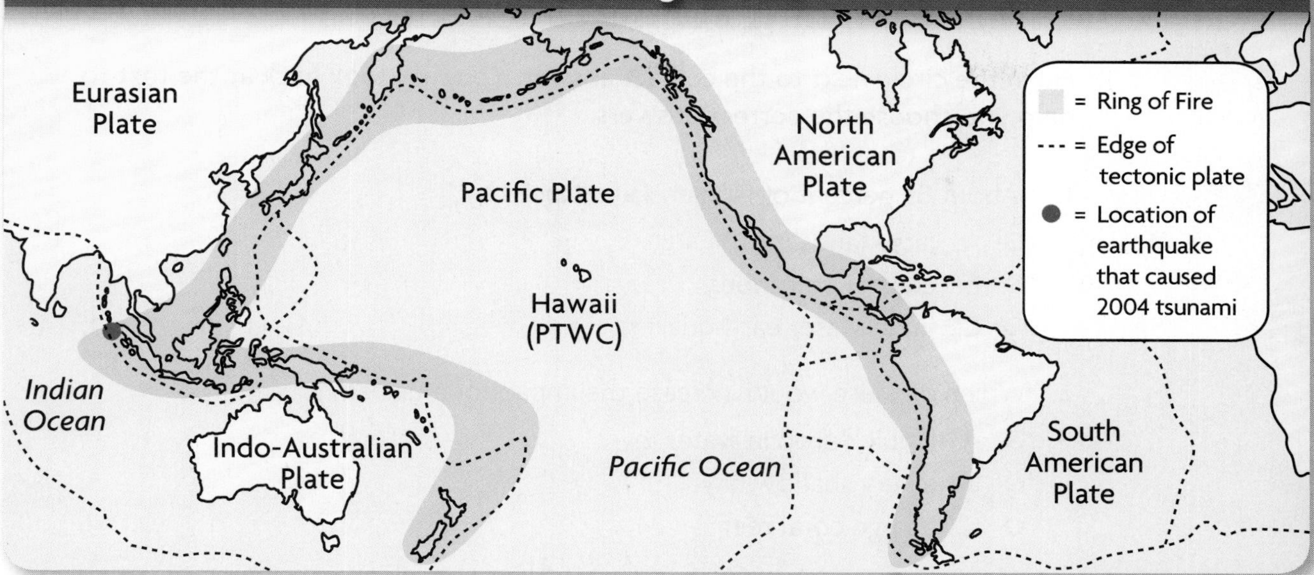

This map shows the area scientists call the Ring of Fire, which runs along the edges of several tectonic plates and is the site of many of Earth's largest earthquakes. The movement of the plates in the Ring of Fire causes many tsunamis in the Pacific Ocean—and in other oceans too. **Think about which ocean was affected during the 2004 tsunami.**

19 Unfortunately, in 2004 none of these gauges had been set up in the Indian Ocean. Scientists detected the 2004 earthquake in the Indian Ocean, but they had no way of knowing if a tsunami was forming or not—until it struck.

20 The United Nations has called for a tsunami warning system to be developed specifically for the Indian Ocean. The organization hopes that this system will be implemented soon, greatly reducing—and possibly eliminating—tsunami-related injuries and fatalities in the area.

Did You Know?

- Tsunami-like waves can also occur in any large, deep lake. These giant waves, called seiches, can slosh back and forth from side to side for hours.
- An earthquake triggered a seiche at Hebgen Lake in Montana in 1959.

Self-Check

Look back at the prediction you wrote on page 80.

- Does your prediction match the text? Why or why not?

Write your answers on a separate sheet of paper.

A

Understanding What You Read

Fill in the circle next to the correct answer. You may look back at the text to help you choose the correct answers.

1. About 85 percent of tsunamis are caused by

- ❍ A. large landslides.
- ❍ B. coastal volcanoes.
- ❍ C. underwater earthquakes.

2. Which of these would increase the impact of a tsunami?

- ❍ A. a quick drop in water level
- ❍ B. a very shallow bay
- ❍ C. a large coral reef

3. From the information in paragraph 16, you can infer that

- ❍ A. a person who grabs and holds onto a strong tree might survive a tsunami.
- ❍ B. most good swimmers wouldn't have any trouble swimming to safety during a tsunami.
- ❍ C. when a tsunami first hits land, rescue teams can come in and help people right away.

4. What problem does placing special wave gauges in the ocean solve for scientists who try to predict tsunamis?

- ❍ A. Not all earthquakes cause tsunamis.
- ❍ B. Tides can affect underwater equipment.
- ❍ C. Some landforms make tsunamis stronger.

5. From the map titled "The Ring of Fire," you can conclude that

- ❍ A. the Ring of Fire only affects countries that border the Pacific Ocean.
- ❍ B. Hawaii's location makes it a dangerous place for tsunamis.
- ❍ C. North and South America don't have many earthquakes.

Score 4 points for each correct answer.

_________/20 **Total Score: Activity A**

B

Finding the Main Idea and Details and Visualizing

Paragraph 9 from the article is shown below. Read the paragraph. Then use the paragraph to complete the activities.

Waves consist of high points, called crests, and low points, called troughs. In deep water, far out at sea, the waves aren't very tall. In fact, ships can pass over them without anyone aboard noticing anything unusual. That's because the push of the displaced water sends most of the tsunami's energy outward through the water, not upward toward the surface. The waves of the 2004 tsunami were only two feet (0.6 meter) high in deep water.

1. Fill in the circle next to the sentence that **best** states the main idea of the paragraph.

- ❍ A. Waves consist of high points and low points.
- ❍ B. Tsunami waves aren't very tall in deep water.
- ❍ C. The displaced water goes outward instead of upward.

2. Use the details in the paragraph and what you already know to visualize a ship passing over the waves of a tsunami. Draw what you are visualizing in the box below.

Score 5 points each for numbers 1 and 2.

________ /10 **Total Score: Activity B**

C

Using Words

Complete each sentence with a word from the box. Write the missing word on the line.

misconception	**displaces**	**instantaneous**
intensify	**notorious**	

1. Our neighbor is ______________________ for running his lawn mower at six o'clock on Saturday mornings.

2. The loud noises caused her headache to ______________________.

3. The false information in the article created a ______________________ about what had really happened.

4. The pressure of my hand against the balloon ______________________ the air inside it, causing the balloon to change shape.

5. When he heard the good news, he felt ______________________ relief and smiled for the first time all day.

Choose one word from the box. Write a new sentence using the word. Be sure to put at least one detail in your sentence. The detail should show that you understand what the word means. Use the sentences above as examples.

6. ____

____

Score 4 points for each correct answer in numbers 1–5.
(Do not score number 6.)

________ /20 **Total Score: Activity C**

D

Writing About It

Write a Summary Write a summary of the tsunami article. Finish the sentences below to write your summary. Be sure your summary includes the most important ideas from the article. Use the checklist on page 119 to check your work.

A tsunami is ______________________________

____

____

When the water is displaced, ______________________________

____

____

When a tsunami hits land, ______________________________

____

____

The waves of a tsunami ______________________________

____

____

To predict when a tsunami might occur, ______________________________

____

____

____

Lesson 7 Add your scores from activities A, B, and C to get your total score.

_______ **A** Understanding What You Read

_______ **B** Finding the Main Idea and Details and Visualizing

_______ **C** Using Words

_______ **Total Score**

Multiply your **Total Score x 2** _______

This is your percentage score.

Record your percentage score on the graph on page 121.

Hydrothermal Vents
A Dark, Mysterious World

Hydrothermal (hī′-drə-thər′-məl) vents make life possible in the cold, dark world of the ocean's depths.

LESSON 8

READING SKILL

Reviewing the Reading Skills

You practiced three reading skills in Unit Two. Rate your understanding of each skill using the chart below. Use the following rating scale:

3 I understand this skill well. I use it easily and correctly while I read.

2 I understand this skill a little bit. I sometimes use it correctly while I read.

1 I don't understand this skill. I am not able to use it while I read.

Mark the box under the number 3, 2, or 1 for each skill.

	3	**2**	**1**	**Need to review?**		**Turn to:**
Making Connections				Yes	No	Lesson 4, page 41
Asking Questions				Yes	No	Lesson 5, page 53
Making Inferences				Yes	No	Lesson 6, page 65

If you rated your understanding of a skill at 2 or 1, look back at the lesson page where that skill was taught. The lesson page is shown in the chart above. Reread the skill definition and the example. This will help you get ready to complete the next lesson.

After you have reviewed the skills, complete the sentences below.

The skill I find most helpful when reading is ____________________

because ____________________

____

During this lesson, one thing I can do to improve my reading is ____________________

____

____

Getting Ready to Read

Think About What You Know

CONNECT Think about what life might be like in the deepest parts of the ocean. What do you know about the floor of the ocean and the creatures that live there? Write your answers here.

____

____

____

Word Power

PREVIEW Read the words and definitions below. Then look ahead at the title and at the headings and images in the article.

bizarre (bə-zär′)	very unusual or odd
buoyant (boi′-ənt)	able to float
inhospitable (in′-hä-spi′-tə-bəl)	providing no shelter or food
viable (vī′-ə-bəl)	able to function in a satisfactory way
speculate (spe′-kyə-lāt′)	to think that something might be true even though it has not yet been proven

QUESTION Use the words, title, headings, and images to ask a question. What would you like to know about hydrothermal vents? Write your question on the lines below.

____

____

____

Reason to Read

Read to find out if the information in the text answers your question. At the end of the article, you will be asked to look back at your question. You will decide whether or not your question is answered in the text.

Hydrothermal Vents
A Dark, Mysterious World

1 The creatures are like nothing you've ever seen. They include giant worms, eyeless shrimp, and fish with no scales. These **bizarre** life-forms live in a dark world of extreme heat, bitter cold, and pressure that would squash a human like a bug.

2 This is not some weird planet dreamed up by a science fiction writer. Rather, it describes a place found right here on Earth: the world of hydrothermal vents at the bottom of the ocean.

Cracks in the Earth

3 Perhaps you've heard of Old Faithful, a famous geyser in Wyoming. A geyser is a type of hot spring that periodically erupts into the air, shooting out water and gases that have been heated deep inside the earth. A hydrothermal vent is like a geyser, but it's located deep underwater on the ocean floor.

4 Researchers discovered the first hydrothermal vent in 1977 in the Pacific Ocean. Scientists have since found more than 200 clusters of vents (called vent fields) around the world. Most are located along the ridges of a 40,000-mile-long (64,374 km) undersea mountain chain that snakes around the globe.

5 Along the chain Earth's massive tectonic plates slowly shift, creating small cracks in the ocean floor between the plates. Cold seawater gets sucked down through some of the cracks and plunges a mile or two below the ocean floor, where it's exposed to hot **magma.** The magma **superheats** the water to temperatures as high as 750°F (400°C). This makes the water **buoyant,** so it shoots back up through other cracks. These cracks—which range in size from half an inch to six feet (1 cm to 183 cm) wide—are the vents.

---

magma (mag′-mə) hot melted rock beneath the surface of the earth
superheats (so͞o′-pər-hēts′) heats a liquid beyond its regular boiling point without boiling it

My WORKSPACE

To explore the ocean's depths, scientists cram themselves into underwater vehicles designed to withstand the pressures of the deep. **Think about how it would feel to be in this machine on the ocean floor.**

Connect

Use the information in **paragraph 5** to make a connection. Try to make your connection a text-to-text or text-to-world connection. Complete the sentence below.

When I read about ______

______

______

it reminds me ______

______

______

because ______

______

______

What type of connection did you make? You may look back at page 41 if you need help.

______

My WORKSPACE

Infer

Reread the shaded text. Use the information in the text and what you already know to make an inference. Write your inference below.

___

___

___

___

Is this a small or big inference? How do you know? Write your answers below.

___

___

___

___

How Hydrothermal Vents Form

1. Cold water seeps down through cracks.
2. Water, heated by magma, picks up minerals.
3. Buoyant water floats up through other openings.
4. Metals and other substances cause water to appear black and smoky.

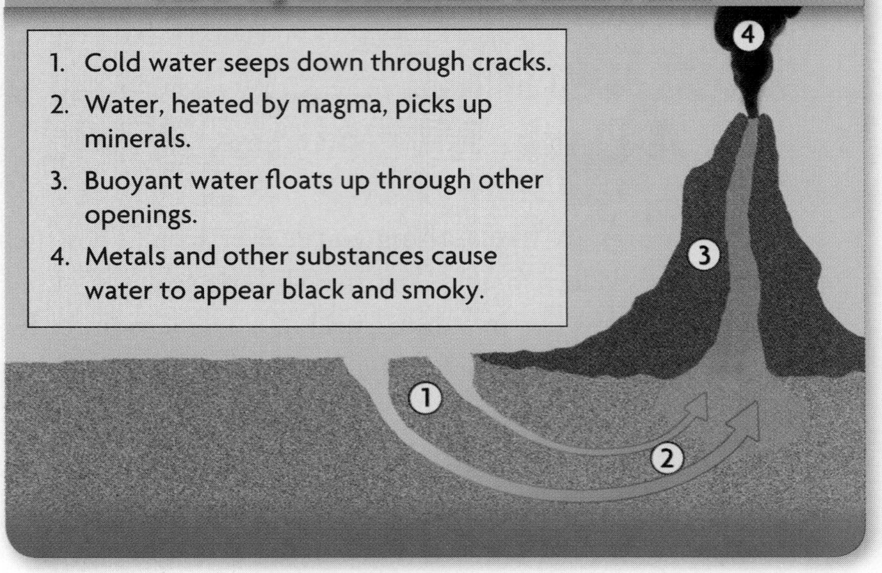

Metals and minerals in heated seawater mix with other substances, producing a black smoker hydrothermal vent. **Think about the difference in temperature between the water leaving the vent and the water surrounding it.**

6 But even though the erupting water is extremely hot, it isn't boiling. At sea level, water boils at 212°F (100°C), but at great depths, the weight of the ocean above is so intense that water cannot boil unless it reaches temperatures much greater than the 750°F (400°C) of the vent water.

Where There's Smoke, There's Water

7 While it's below the ocean floor, the water picks up metals and minerals from the rock inside the earth. When the water erupts from the vent, these compounds cause a reaction that makes the water appear black, earning these vents the name "black smokers." (There are also "white smokers," which are lower-temperature vents that release white, metal-free water.)

8 After the compounds shoot up into the ocean, they fall back toward the ocean floor and collect on top of one another, forming long, thin columns called chimneys. Chimneys can grow more than a foot (.3 meter) per month, reaching great heights before collapsing under the pressure of their own weight. One vent chimney in the Pacific Ocean, nicknamed "Godzilla," grew 135 feet (41 meters) high, toppled over, and began to grow again.

9 But as fascinating as the vents themselves are, the creatures that live near them are even more intriguing.

In Too Deep

10 To truly appreciate the life-forms that live in this environment, you need to realize just how **inhospitable** the conditions are down there. For starters, the pressure of the weight of the ocean would crush most organisms, and the chemicals in the superheated water are toxic to most life on our planet. Then there is the stark contrast of temperatures, often just inches apart—the deep-sea water temperature hovers around a bitter 36°F (2°C), only a few degrees above freezing, but it shoots to scalding extremes in the area immediately around hydrothermal vents.

11 Perhaps the biggest challenge to the existence of life at the bottom of the ocean, however, is the absence of sunlight. Because sunlight can't penetrate beyond a few hundred feet into the ocean, hydrothermal vents exist in permanent darkness.

12 Scientists used to firmly believe that sunlight was crucial to all life on Earth because animals rely on plants or on other plant-eating animals for their food, and plants get their energy from sunlight. It follows that if the sun were removed from the equation, the entire **food chain** would be disrupted and life could not sustain itself.

13 So imagine scientists' surprise when, upon discovering this sunless world of hydrothermal vents, they also discovered more than 300 species of animals living there! Most of these animals, including some species of snails, crabs, and octopi, were previously unknown to humans.

food chain (fo͞od′-chān′) the way life-forms eat and are eaten by other life-forms

My WORKSPACE

Ask Questions

Reread **paragraph 10.** What question would you like to ask about the information in this paragraph? Write your question on the lines below.

____

____

____

How does asking this question help you stay interested in the text as you read?

____

____

____

____

My WORKSPACE

No Light? No Problem!

14 The discovery of an entire **ecosystem** existing in the absence of sunlight provided quite a challenge for scientists. They had to expand their thinking to understand how this incredible phenomenon works.

15 They discovered that a hydrothermal vent ecosystem functions with a process very similar to photosynthesis, the process by which plants convert sunlight's energy into food. But the foundations of the food chain in a vent ecosystem are chemicals and bacteria instead of sunlight and plants. Although the chemicals emerging from the vents are poisonous to most organisms on Earth, certain bacteria in and around the vents are able to convert them into food and energy through a process called chemosynthesis. These bacteria are the root of the ecosystem's food chain. They grow together to form thick mats around the vents, and other creatures graze on them directly.

16 Some animals, rather than eating the bacteria or the bacteria-eaters, use the bacteria in another way. One example is the tube worm, which can grow up to eight feet (2.4 meters) long and has no mouth, eyes, or stomach. It survives by allowing the bacteria to live inside its body. The worm uses a body part called a plume to take compounds from the water into its body, and the bacteria convert these chemicals into food for the worm.

Life Is Tough!

17 As you can see, there is a **viable** food chain in this ecosystem. But how do the creatures deal with the other brutal challenges of this environment? Like life-forms all over the planet, they've adapted to their surroundings. For example, living creatures with air pockets such as lungs would be crushed at that depth because the pressure would flatten the air pockets. The intense pressure does not bother vent animals, however. Their bodies evolved without air spaces, so the pressure does not flatten them.

ecosystem (ē'-kō-sis'-təm) the life-forms in a particular area, and how they relate to each other and to the place in which they live

Infer

Reread the shaded text. Use the information in the text and what you already know to make an inference. Write your inference below.

Is this a small or big inference? How do you know? Write your answers below.

Some scientists say that the bacteria in the "furry" claws of a yeti crab help make the surrounding water less poisonous to the crab. **Think about why yeti crabs and many other vent creatures are white in color.**

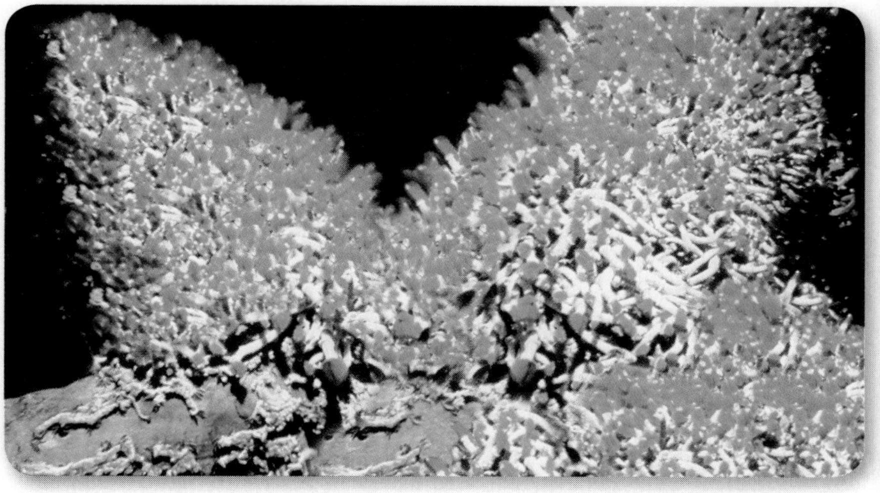

Giant tube worms lodge one end of their bodies in the ocean floor and let the other end wave in the water like grass. The red waving ends are the plumes, which fill with blood that transfers the compounds they collect to the bacteria. **Think about why the worms lodge one end of their bodies in the ocean floor.**

18 As for the temperature extremes, the cold is a minor challenge compared to the intense heat near the vent. Mystery still shrouds how some of these creatures survive the hot water. But scientists **speculate** that some animals, such as certain types of worms, are able to tolerate the scalding water of the vents by allowing heat-resistant bacteria to coat their bodies.

19 Given their amazing ability to survive such harsh conditions, vent creatures continue to be a source of fascination for scientists. Some believe they hold promise for new medical treatments, and others are convinced that, because the bacteria can consume some harmful chemicals, they might be useful in cleaning up toxic waste. So the remarkable undersea world of hydrothermal vents might someday help our surface world become a healthier, cleaner place to live.

My WORKSPACE

Connect

Use the information in **paragraph 19** to make a connection. Try to make your connection a text-to-text or text-to-world connection. Complete the sentence below.

When I read about ________

____

____

it reminds me ________

____

____

because ________

____

____

What type of connection did you make?

____

Self-Check

Look back at the question you wrote on page 92.

- Does the information in the text answer your question? If it does, what is the answer? If it does not, where could you look to find more information?

Write your answers on a separate sheet of paper.

A

Understanding What You Read

Fill in the circle next to the correct answer. You may look back at the text to help you choose the correct answers.

1. Under which heading would you be **most likely** to find information about how hydrothermal vents form from splits in the ocean floor?

- ❍ A. Life Is Tough!
- ❍ B. Cracks in the Earth
- ❍ C. No Light? No Problem!

2. The diagram titled "How Hydrothermal Vents Form" helps support the author's point that

- ❍ A. magma heats the seawater when it's below the ocean floor.
- ❍ B. the weight of the ocean creates a lot of pressure.
- ❍ C. one vent chimney is nicknamed "Godzilla."

3. While it's below the ocean floor, the water picks up

- ❍ A. clouds of black smoke.
- ❍ B. bacteria from the worms' skin.
- ❍ C. metals and minerals from the rock.

4. Which of these statements **best** summarizes the information in the "In Too Deep" section?

- ❍ A. Scientists were amazed to discover that life exists near hydrothermal vents despite intense pressure, extreme temperatures, and darkness.
- ❍ B. Scientists discovered more than 300 previously unknown species of creatures living near hydrothermal vents.
- ❍ C. Scientists used to believe that life would be unable to sustain itself without sunlight.

5. How does chemosynthesis solve the problem of the absence of sunlight?

- ❍ A. It allows plants to convert sunlight into food.
- ❍ B. It allows bacteria to convert chemicals into food.
- ❍ C. It allows vent creatures to convert magma into food.

Score 4 points for each correct answer.

_________/20 **Total Score: Activity A**

B

Making Connections and Making Inferences

Paragraph 12 from the article is shown below. Read the paragraph. Then use the paragraph to complete the activities.

Scientists used to firmly believe that sunlight was crucial to all life on Earth because animals rely on plants or on other plant-eating animals for their food, and plants get their energy from sunlight. It follows that if the sun were removed from the equation, the entire food chain would be disrupted and life could not sustain itself.

1. Complete the sentence to make a connection to the paragraph above.

When I read about ______________________________

____

it reminds me ______________________________

____

because ______________________________

____

2. Use the information in the paragraph to make an inference. You can also use the connection you made above to help you make your inference. Write your inference on the lines below. Then explain why it's a big or small inference.

____

____

____

This is a ______________ inference because ______________

____

____

Score 5 points each for numbers 1 and 2.

________ /10 **Total Score: Activity B**

C

Using Words

Complete the analogies below by writing a word from the box on each line. Remember that in an analogy, the last two words must be related in the same way that the first two are related.

bizarre	**buoyant**	**inhospitable**
viable	**speculate**	

1. escape : flee : : guess : ______

2. knife : sharp : : boat : ______

3. spotless : filthy : : ordinary : ______

4. massive : tiny : : welcoming : ______

5. enthusiastic : eager : : workable : ______

Choose one word from the box. Write a sentence using the word. Be sure to put at least one detail in your sentence. The detail should show that you understand what the word means.

6. ______

______

Score 4 points for each correct answer in numbers 1–5.
(Do not score number 6.)

______ /20 **Total Score: Activity C**

D

Writing About It

Write Interview Questions Suppose you had the chance to interview a scientist who studies hydrothermal vents. Write a list of questions you would want to ask her or him about hydrothermal vents. Begin each question with *who, what, when, where, why,* or *how.* Be sure your writing matches the information in the text. Use the checklist on page 119 to check your work.

1. ______________________________

____

2. ______________________________

____

3. ______________________________

____

4. ______________________________

____

5. ______________________________

____

____

Lesson 8 Add your scores from activities A, B, and C to get your total score.

_______ **A** Understanding What You Read

_______ **B** Making Connections and Making Inferences

_______ **C** Using Words

_______ **Total Score**

Multiply your **Total Score x 2** _______

This is your percentage score.

Record your percentage score on the graph on page 121.

PARASITES

Uninvited Guests

Parasites come in many shapes and sizes, but they all have something in common—they want something from you.

READING SKILL

Reviewing the Reading Skills

You practiced six reading skills in this book. Rate your understanding of each skill using the chart below. Use the following rating scale:

3 I understand this skill well. I use it easily and correctly while I read.

2 I understand this skill a little bit. I sometimes use it correctly while I read.

1 I don't understand this skill. I am not able to use it while I read.

Mark the box under the number 3, 2, or 1 for each skill.

	3	2	1	Need to review?		Turn to:
Visualizing				Yes	No	Lesson 1, page 3
Finding the Main Idea and Details				Yes	No	Lesson 2, page 15
Summarizing				Yes	No	Lesson 3, page 27
Making Connections				Yes	No	Lesson 4, page 41
Asking Questions				Yes	No	Lesson 5, page 53
Making Inferences				Yes	No	Lesson 6, page 65

If you rated your understanding of a skill at 2 or 1, look back at the lesson page where that skill was taught. The lesson page is shown in the chart above. Reread the skill definition and the example. This will help you get ready to complete the next lesson. After you have reviewed the skills, complete the sentences below.

The skill I find most helpful when reading is ______________________

because ______________________

____

During this lesson, one thing I can do to improve my reading is ______________________

____

____

Getting Ready to Read

Think About What You Know

CONNECT What do you know about parasites, such as fleas, ticks, and leeches? What do parasites need to do to survive? Write your answers here.

____

____

____

Word Power

PREVIEW Read the words and definitions below. Then look ahead at the title and at the headings and images in the article.

organism (ôr′-gə-ni′-zəm)	a living thing, such as a plant, an animal, or a person
reside (ri-zīd′)	to live in a specific place
infest (in-fest′)	to come together in large amounts and live inside something in a manner that is harmful
extensive (ik-sten′-siv)	large in size or effect
preventive (pri-ven′-tiv)	meant to stop something bad, such as an illness, from happening

PREDICT Use the words, title, headings, and images to make a prediction. What do you think the author will say about parasites?

I predict the author will ____

____

because ____

____

Reason to Read

Read to find out if the prediction you wrote above matches the information in the text. At the end of the article, you will be asked about your prediction. You will need to explain how your prediction is the same as the text or different from it.

PARASITES
Uninvited Guests

1 When Tanya got home from a trip to Costa Rica, she discovered a painful lump on her head. She wasn't concerned—until the lump began to wiggle! A mosquito had deposited an egg from a botfly in Tanya's hair. The egg hatched into a tiny **maggot,** which ate its way into her scalp. A doctor was able to extract it, but Tanya never forgot this encounter with a parasite.

Come On In!

2 A parasite is an **organism** that lives on or inside another organism, using it for food and sometimes shelter. The organism that the parasite uses is called the host. Scientists don't know exactly how many kinds of parasites there are, but they do know that parasites make up the majority of species on Earth. Parasites come in a variety of forms, from **microscopic** single-celled organisms called protozoa to harmless-looking plants to worms several feet long. Parasites utilize plants, animals, or humans as their hosts. This article focuses on parasites that use animals and humans as hosts.

3 Parasites fall into one of two categories. Those that stay on the outside of a host, such as on the skin or in the hair or fur, are called ectoparasites. Fleas and ticks fit into this category. Those that **reside** inside a host's body are called endoparasites. Tapeworms and heartworms are examples of endoparasites.

4 But whether it's *on* the host or *inside* it, a parasite's goal is to steal nourishment from the host. Ectoparasites tend to do this by sucking nutrient-rich blood, while endoparasites often make themselves comfortable in a host's intestines so they can absorb food the host has already digested.

---

maggot (ma'-gət) a tiny worm that will become an insect such as a fly
microscopic (mī'-krə-skä'-pik) extremely small and viewable only through a microscope

My WORKSPACE

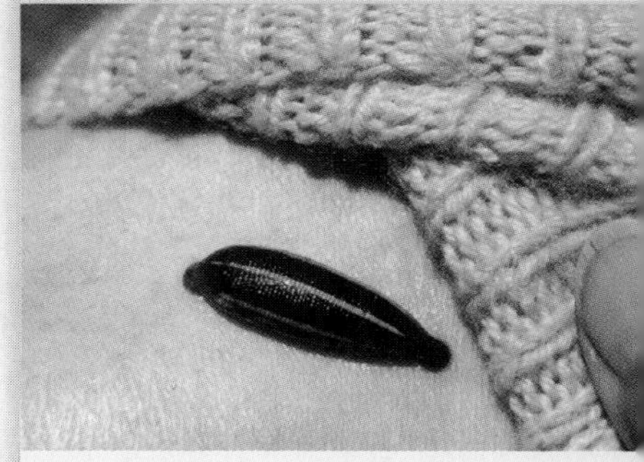

Leeches attach themselves to the outside of a host. **Think about what it is that leeches do that makes them parasites.**

Find the Main Idea

Reread **paragraph 3.** Study the details in the paragraph. Does this paragraph have a topic sentence, or do you need to infer the main idea? Write your answer below.

____

____

What is the main idea of the paragraph?

____

____

____

____

My WORKSPACE

Visualize

Reread **paragraph 6.** Use the details in the text to visualize ectoparasites choosing a host. Draw what you are visualizing in the box below.

How does your visualization help you better understand the text?

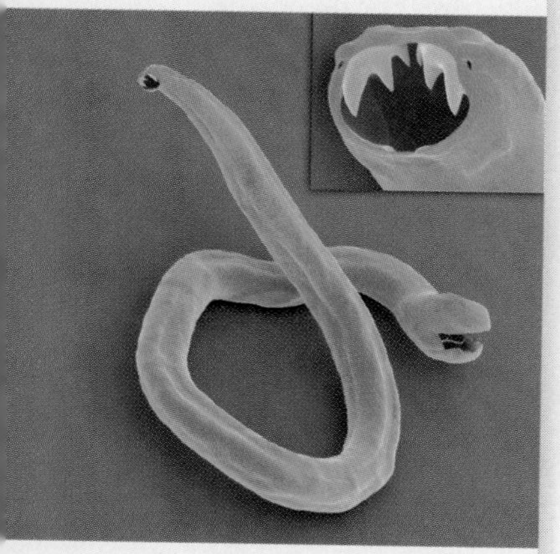

Think about why a hookworm's teeth are so sharp.

5 How do parasites first gain access to their hosts? The answer is that they use all sorts of sneaky ways to accomplish this.

Make Yourself at Home

6 Basically, parasites make sure they're in the right place at the right time. Many ectoparasites simply bide their time in the grass until they can jump onto a passing host, as a tick does with a hiker in the woods. Some might even jump from host to host if the opportunity arises.

7 Endoparasites, on the other hand, need to find an entrance into the host's body. One way they do this is by penetrating the host's skin. A hookworm, for instance, hangs out in soil until an animal or a barefoot person walks on it. Then the worm grabs onto the sole of the foot and burrows through it, making its roundabout way to the host's intestines.

8 Other endoparasites find their way to a host's intestines by getting swallowed. Parasites often live in or lay eggs on meat and other kinds of food, and some can **infest** drinking water areas such as lakes or reservoirs. If an animal or a person consumes contaminated food or water, the parasite gains an easy route to the host's intestines.

Need or Greed?

9 How reliant a parasite is on its host depends on what type of parasite it is. Obligate parasites rely completely on a host to be able to complete their **life cycle.** Once they enter their host, they stay in the same host for their entire lives. However, some of them reproduce outside the host. Some adult worms, for instance, release their eggs within the host's body, but the eggs leave the body through the host's waste. The eggs can lie dormant in the soil for months until, say, a person swallows them while biting fingernails after digging in the garden. Once inside a host, the eggs hatch and the worm's life cycle begins anew.

life cycle (līf′-sī′-kəl) the different stages an animal or a plant goes through during its life

My WORKSPACE

10 Temporary parasites, such as fleas and ticks, require the host for food but can survive without attaching permanently to the host. They may simply grab a quick meal and then hop off (or let go), living on their own until they're hungry again.

11 Facultative parasites can survive without the help of a host, but they will snatch a little treat from a host if they get the opportunity. Consider freshwater leeches. They swim independently in swamps and lakes, and they feed on small creatures and decaying animal matter. But when a host approaches, a leech might latch onto its skin just to get a little extra nourishment.

Little Creatures, Big Trouble

12 Draining a bit of blood or stealing tiny amounts of nutrients from a host's body might not seem like something to be concerned about, but the fact is that a parasite can cause **extensive** harm to its host. A parasite that constantly feeds can weaken a host's body, making the host more vulnerable to disease. Some parasites can also cause additional health problems such as diarrhea, which can result in dangerous **dehydration** and even death.

Ask Questions

Reread **paragraph 12.** What question would you like to ask about the information in this paragraph? Write your question on the lines below.

How does asking this question help you stay interested in the text?

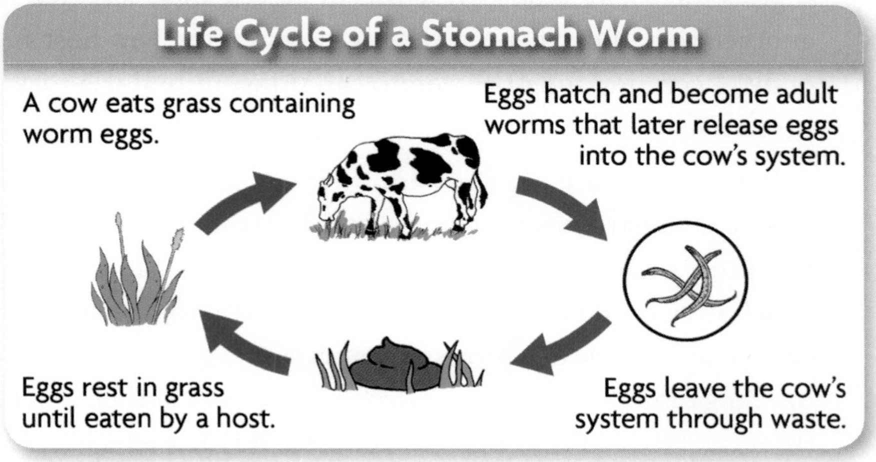

Life Cycle of a Stomach Worm
A cow eats grass containing worm eggs.
Eggs hatch and become adult worms that later release eggs into the cow's system.
Eggs leave the cow's system through waste.
Eggs rest in grass until eaten by a host.

Stomach worms live their adult lives inside a host, but their eggs often leave the host's body and are picked up by other hosts. **Think about why farm animals might be more likely than people to consume parasite eggs.**

dehydration (dē'-hī'-drā'-shən) the loss of fluids from the body

My WORKSPACE

Infer

Reread the shaded text. Use the information in the text and what you already know to make an inference. Write your inference below.

Is this a small or big inference? How do you know? Write your answers below.

Reported Cases of Lyme Disease in the United States

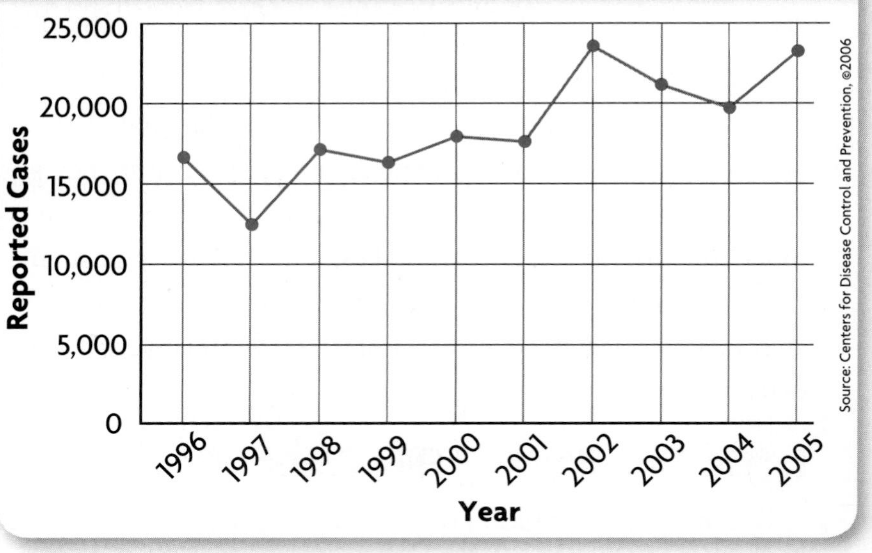

Almost 200,000 cases of Lyme disease, which is transmitted by ticks, have been reported in the United States over a 10-year period. **Think about what might have caused the rise and fall of reported cases over the years.**

13 Some ectoparasites are particularly threatening because they can transfer disease-causing bacteria to a host. For example, a tick that takes blood from a host infected with Lyme disease ingests the bacteria that cause this disease. When that tick bites another host, it can deposit the bacteria into the new host's body. A certain kind of mosquito can transmit **malaria** to a person in a similar manner.

14 But parasites usually don't kill their hosts. This is especially true of endoparasites: if the host perishes, the parasite perishes too. One of several exceptions to this rule is the hairworm, which lives inside grasshoppers. When a hairworm reaches a certain age, it releases proteins that cause its grasshopper host to plunge into water, where it drowns. The worm then emerges from the host into the water to continue its life cycle.

malaria (mə-ler′-ē-ə) a dangerous disease that causes chills and fever and can result in death

Fight Back

15 You might think that it's rare for a person to host a parasite, but scientists estimate that up to 25 percent of the world's population—including 700,000 people in the United States—are currently hosting hookworms and that 1.5 billion people are hosting roundworms. One reason some endoparasites are tough to combat is because they deceive your body into thinking that they're a natural part of it, so your immune system doesn't realize it should destroy them.

16 So how can you fight back against parasites? Sometimes medicines or herbal treatments do the trick, either killing the parasites or flushing them from your body. Some parasites can only be removed surgically, and for some there is no treatment at all.

17 The best strategy is to reduce the likelihood that you will acquire parasites. There are several **preventive** measures you can take:

- Make sure to wash fresh fruits and vegetables and to properly cook foods such as meat.
- Do not drink water from rivers or lakes unless you treat it with special equipment such as a water filter.
- When you're outdoors, use insect repellent and wear shoes—especially in areas where animals live.
- Wash your hands frequently.

By carefully following these basic guidelines, you significantly reduce your chances of acquiring a dangerous—or just plain gross—parasite.

My WORKSPACE

Summarize

Sometimes you may need to summarize text that is several paragraphs long. Review the "Fight Back" section. Write the **three** most important ideas in this section.

1. ____________________

2. ____________________

3. ____________________

Now use these three ideas to write a summary of the section. Remember that your summary should be about 20 words or less.

____

____

____

____

____

Self-Check

Look back at the prediction you wrote on page 104.

- Does your prediction match the text? Why or why not?

Write your answers on a separate sheet of paper.

A

Understanding What You Read

Fill in the circle next to the correct answer. You may look back at the text to help you choose the correct answers.

1. Whether it's on the host or inside it, a parasite's goal is to

- ❍ A. transfer disease-causing bacteria.
- ❍ B. steal nourishment from the host.
- ❍ C. trick a body's immune system.

2. Which of these parasites can survive without any help from a host?

- ❍ A. fleas
- ❍ B. ticks
- ❍ C. leeches

3. The diagram titled "Life Cycle of a Stomach Worm" helps support the author's point that some worms

- ❍ A. release eggs within the host's body.
- ❍ B. enter a host by penetrating the skin.
- ❍ C. might infect as many as 700,000 people in the United States.

4. Which step has to happen **before** an ectoparasite can transfer a disease to a host?

- ❍ A. The current host dies from the disease.
- ❍ B. The parasite bites a host already infected with the disease.
- ❍ C. The worm lays eggs that pass out of the host's body in the waste.

5. Ectoparasites and endoparasites are similar because they both

- ❍ A. jump easily from host to host.
- ❍ B. travel to a host's intestines.
- ❍ C. usually don't kill their hosts.

Score 4 points for each correct answer.

_______ /20 **Total Score: Activity A**

B

Finding the Main Idea and Details and Making Inferences

Paragraph 13 from the article is shown below. Read the paragraph. Then use the paragraph to complete the activities.

Some ectoparasites are particularly threatening because they can transfer disease-causing bacteria to a host. For example, a tick that takes blood from a host infected with Lyme disease ingests the bacteria that cause this disease. When that tick bites another host, it can deposit the bacteria into the new host's body. A certain kind of mosquito can transmit malaria to a person in a similar manner.

1. Fill in the circle next to the sentence that **best** states the main idea of the paragraph.

- ○ A. Ticks and mosquitoes are dangerous insects.
- ○ B. Some parasites can transmit a disease to a host.
- ○ C. Some hosts carry disease-causing bacteria in their bodies.

2. Use the information in the paragraph and what you already know to make an inference. Write your inference on the lines below. Then explain why it's a small or big inference.

____

____

____

This is a ____________________ inference because ____________________

____

____

Score 5 points each for numbers 1 and 2.

________ /10 **Total Score: Activity B**

C

Using Words

Follow the instructions below. Write your answers on the lines.

1. List **three** examples of an **organism** found in the ocean.

____

____

____

2. List **two** types of buildings where people might **reside.**

____

____

3. List **two** creatures that might **infest** a home.

____

____

4. List **two** events in nature that can cause **extensive** damage.

____

____

5. List **two** things parents of young children do that are **preventive.**

____

____

Score 4 points for each correct answer.

_______ /20 **Total Score: Activity C**

D

Writing About It

Write a Summary Write a summary of the article you just read about parasites. Finish the sentences below to write your summary. Be sure your summary includes the most important ideas from the article. Use the checklist on page 119 to check your work.

Parasites are ____

____

____

Parasites gain access to their hosts by ___________________________

____

____

Some parasites rely completely on their hosts, while others __________

____

____

Parasites can be harmful because ________________________________

____

____

To protect themselves against parasites, people should _______

____

____

____

Lesson 9 Add your scores from activities A, B, and C to get your total score.

______ **A** Understanding What You Read

______ **B** Finding the Main Idea and Details and Making Inferences

______ **C** Using Words

______ **Total Score**

Multiply your **Total Score x 2** ______

This is your percentage score.

Record your percentage score on the graph on page 121.

UNIT THREE
WRAP-UP

Compare and Contrast

You read three articles about nature in Unit Three. Think about the topic of each article. Then choose **two** of the articles. Write the titles of the articles in the first two boxes below. Draw pictures in the first two boxes that show how the topics are different. In the bottom box, draw a picture that shows how the topics are similar. Label the important parts of your drawings.

Title ______________________________

Title ______________________________

Both

Use your drawings to write a summary of how these nature topics are alike and different. Finish the sentences below to write your summary.

______________ and ______________ are different

because ______________________________

____

______________ and ______________ are similar

because ______________________________

____

Glossary

A

altered (ôl′-tərd) changed in some way *p. 57*

aroma (ə-rō′-mə) a strong, pleasing smell *p. 45*

array (ə-rā′) a group of things that is impressive because of its size, quality, or variety *p. 31*

assert (ə-sərt′) to state strongly and positively *p. 68*

authentic (ə-then′-tik) real or genuine *p. 9*

B

bizarre (bə-zär′) very unusual or odd *p. 93*

buoyant (boi′-ənt) able to float *p. 93*

C

comparable (käm′-prə-bəl) alike enough to be compared *p. 70*

conventional (kən-vench′-nəl) following accepted standards or customs *p. 67*

convey (kən-vā′) to communicate *p. 8*

cumbersome (kəm′-bər-səm) not easily managed or carried *p. 19*

D

deteriorates (di-tir′-ē-ə-rāts′) becomes worse in condition *p. 56*

disadvantages (dis′-əd-van′-tij-əz) conditions that cause problems or that make it hard to succeed *p. 56*

displaces (dis-plās′-əz) moves something from its usual place or position *p. 81*

E

extensive (ik-sten′-siv) large in size or effect *p. 107*

Technology

Food

I

indefinitely (in-de'-fə-nət-lē) for a period of time with no clear ending *p. 56*

infest (in-fest') to come together in large amounts and live inside something in a manner that is harmful *p. 106*

ingenious (in-jēn'-yəs) very clever; very good at inventing new things *p. 33*

ingenuity (in'-jə-no͞o'-ə-tē) the skill to invent or imagine new things *p. 7*

inhospitable (in'-hä-spi'-tə-bəl) providing no shelter or food *p. 95*

initiating (i-ni'-shē-āt'-ing) starting something *p. 44*

instantaneous (in'-stən-tā'-nē-əs) occurring immediately *p. 82*

intensify (in-ten'-sə-fī') to make something greater or stronger *p. 83*

interprets (in-tər'-prəts) finds and understands the meaning of something *p. 18*

intrinsic (in-trin'-zik) being part of the essential nature of something *p. 31*

M

maturity (mə-cho͞or'-ə-tē) the state of being fully grown or developed *p. 43*

misconception (mis'-kən-sep'-shən) a false or mistaken idea *p. 81*

modify (mä'-də-fī') to make minor changes to something *p. 44*

motivated (mō'-tə-vāt'-əd) inspired someone or something to take action *p. 30*

N

notorious (nō-tôr'-ē-əs) well known for a bad or unpleasant reason *p. 84*

O

organism (ôr′-gə-ni′-zəm) a living thing, such as a plant, an animal, or a person *p. 105*

P

palatable (pa′-lə-tə-bəl) having an agreeable taste *p. 47*

precision (pri-si′-zhən) the quality of being very accurate or exact *p. 19*

preventive (pri-ven′-tiv) meant to stop something bad, such as an illness, from happening *p. 109*

R

recipients (ri-si′-pē-ənts) people who receive or take something that is given or offered to them *p. 20*

reside (ri-zīd′) to live in a specific place *p. 105*

S

sanitary (sa′-nə-ter′-ē) free of dirt and germs that can be harmful to health *p. 69*

significant (sig-ni′-fi-kənt) having special value, importance, or meaning *p. 5*

simultaneously (sī′-məl-tā′-nē-əs-lē) at the same time *p. 21*

situated (si′-chə-wāt′-əd) located in a specific place *p. 30*

sophisticated (sə-fis′-tə-kā′-təd) advanced, complex, or well designed *p. 8*

speculate (spe′-kyə-lāt′) to think that something might be true even though it has not yet been proven *p. 97*

sterile (ster′-əl) free from germs *p. 57*

synthetic (sin-the′-tik) composed of human-made substances instead of being found in nature *p. 67*

V

viable (vī′-ə-bəl) able to function in a satisfactory way *p. 96*

Nature

Pronunciation Guide

a	m**a**t	oo	l**oo**k
ä	f**a**ther	o͞o	f**oo**d
ā	d**a**t**e**	oi	n**oi**se
ch	**ch**in	ow	**ou**t
e	w**e**t	ə	penc**i**l
ē	**see**	sh	**s**ugar
i	t**i**p	th	**th**ink
ī	f**i**n**e**	<u>th</u>	**th**em
ng	si**ng**	ū	c**u**t**e**
ô	l**aw**	zh	u**s**ual
ō	**so**		

Writing Checklist

1. I followed the directions for writing.

2. My writing shows that I read and understood the article.

3. I capitalized the names of people.

4. I capitalized the proper names of places and things.

5. I put a punctuation mark at the end of each sentence.

6. I read my writing aloud and listened for missing words.

7. I used a dictionary to check words that didn't look right.

Use the chart below to check off the things on the list that you have done.

√	Lesson Numbers								
Checklist Numbers	1	2	3	4	5	6	7	8	9
1.									
2.									
3.									
4.									
5.									
6.									
7.									

Progress Graph Instructions and Sample

You can take charge of your own progress. The Progress Graph on the next page can help you. Use it to keep track of how you are doing as you work through the lessons in this book. Check the graph often with your teacher. Decide together whether you need to work some more on any of the skills. What types of skills cause you trouble? Talk with your teacher about ways to improve your understanding of these skills.

A sample Progress Graph is shown below. The first three lessons have been filled in to show you how to mark the graph.

Sample Progress Graph

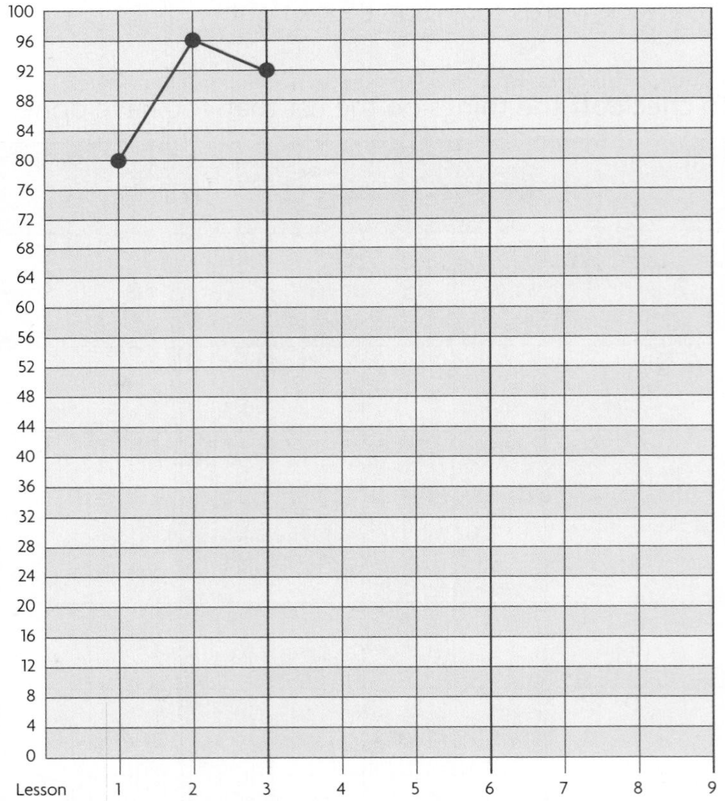

% Score	80	96	92						

Progress Graph

Directions: Write your percentage score for each lesson in the box under the lesson number. Then draw a dot on the line to show your score. Draw the dot above the number of the lesson and across from the score you earned. Graph your progress by drawing a line to connect the dots.

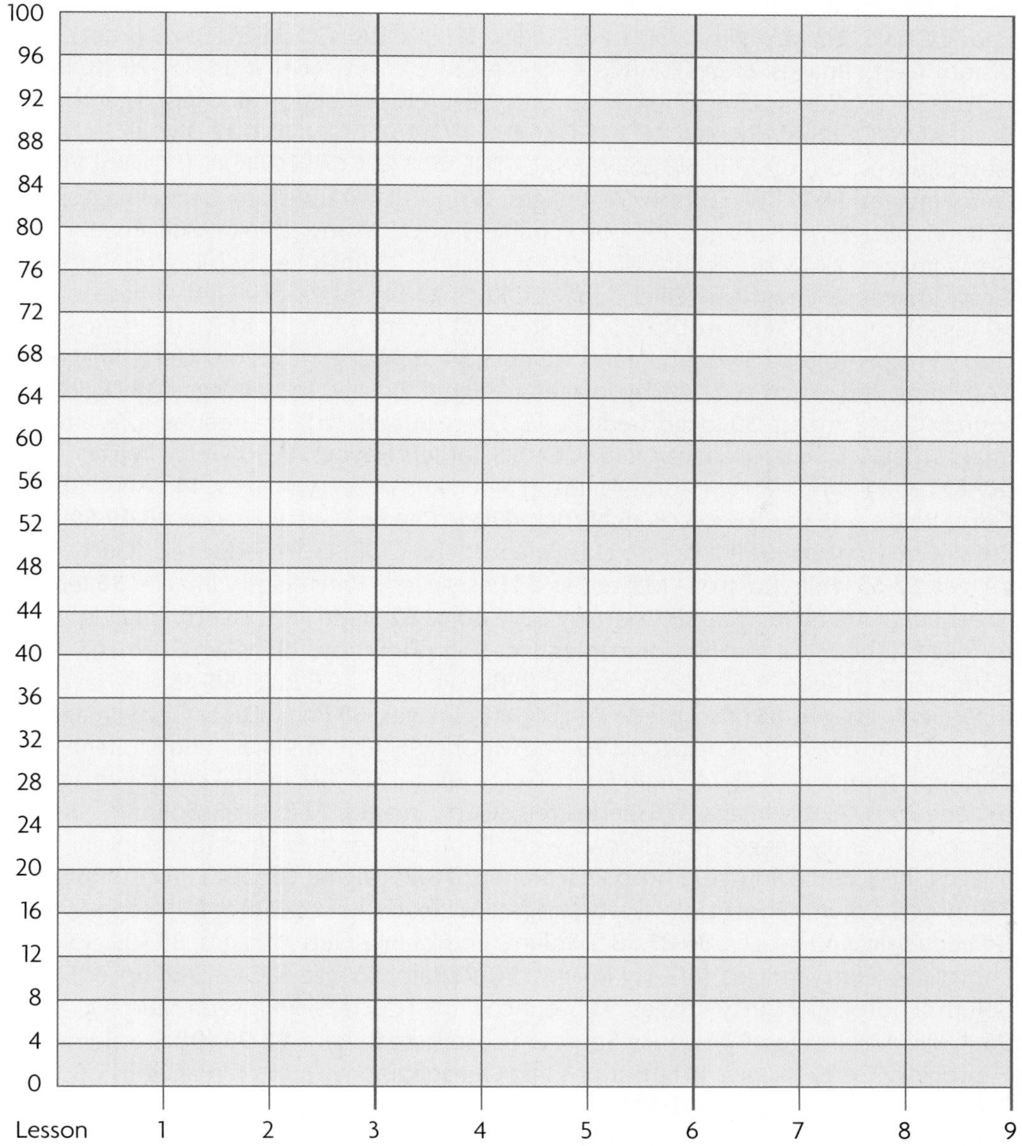

% Score									

Image Credits

Cover (bkgd t)Cartesia/Getty Images, (l)Photodisc/PunchStock, (r)Comstock Images/Alamy Images, (b)Royalty-Free/CORBIS; **i** Cartesia/Getty Images; **iii** (t)Win McNamee/Getty Images, (b)The McGraw-Hill Companies/Lisa Mullenholz; **iv** A. Filis/AP Images; **v** Mary Kate Denny/PhotoEdit; **1** (bkgd)Digital Vision/Getty Images, (tr)Win McNamee/Getty Images, (l)AMBLIN/UNIVERSAL/THE KOBAL COLLECTION, (br)Stephanie Pilick/dpa/CORBIS; **2-3** MARVEL/SONY PICTURES/THE KOBAL COLLECTION; **3** (inset)Digital Vision/Getty Images; **6** CASTLE ROCK/SHANGRI-LA ENTERTAINMENT/THE KOBAL COLLECTION; **7** New Line Cinema/Courtesy: Everett Collection; **8** Joseph Murphy; **9** DREAMWORKS/PARAMOUNT/THE KOBAL COLLECTION; **10 11 12** Digital Vision/Getty Images; **13** (l c)AMBLIN/UNIVERSAL/THE KOBAL COLLECTION, (r)Digital Vision/Getty Images; **14-15** Rob Griffith/AP Images; **15** (inset)Digital Vision/Getty Images; **17** Karen Nichols/AP Images; **19** Photo courtesy of U.S. Army; **21** Win McNamee/Getty Images; **22 23 24** Digital Vision/Getty Images; **25** (l)Pat Lewis, (r)Digital Vision/Getty Images; **26** Stephanie Pilick/dpa/CORBIS; **27** Digital Vision/Getty Images; **30** Joseph Murphy; **31** PhotoDisc/SuperStock; **32** Joseph Murphy; **33** (t)Ed Freeman/Getty Images, (b)Brad Swonetz/zefa/CORBIS; **34 35 36** Digital Vision/Getty Images; **37** (l)PhotosIndia.com LLC/Alamy Images, (r)Digital Vision/Getty Images; **38** Digital Vision/Getty Images; **39** (bkgd)Siede Preis/Getty Images, (tr)Jeff Greenberg/Alamy Images, (l)JLP/Jose Luis Pelaez/zefa/CORBIS, (br)Jeff Haynes/AFP/Getty Images; **40-41** Tetra Images/PunchStock; **41** (inset) Siede Preis/Getty Images; **44** PANAPRESS/Getty Images; **45** StockFood/PunchStock; **47** Joe Raedle/Getty Images; **48 49 50** Siede Preis/Getty Images; **51** (l)JLP/Jose Luis Pelaez/zefa/CORBIS, (r)Siede Preis/Getty Images; **52-53** Philip Rostron/Masterfile; **53** (inset)Siede Preis/Getty Images; **56** Jeff Greenberg/Alamy Images; **58** Courtesy FDA; **60 61 62** Siede Preis/Getty Images; **63** (bkgd t)The McGraw-Hill Companies, Inc./John Flournoy, (c)The McGraw-Hill Companies, (r)Siede Preis/Getty Images, (b)Royalty-Free/CORBIS; **64-65** Jeff Haynes/AFP/Getty Images; **65** (inset)Siede Preis/Getty Images; **68** PhotoDisc/Getty Images; **69** Scott Barrow, Inc./SuperStock; **70** The McGraw-Hill Companies/Lisa Mullenholz; **71** Joseph Murphy; **72 73 74** Siede Preis/Getty Images; **75** (l)Marc Hill/Alamy Images, (r)Siede Preis/Getty Images; **76** Siede Preis/Getty Images; **77** (bkgd)S. Solum/PhotoLink/Getty Images, (tr)Andrew Syred/Photo Researchers, Inc., (l)Bedu Saini/AP Images, (br)Science Source/Photo Researchers; **78-79** Digital Globe/EPA/CORBIS; **79** (inset)S. Solum/PhotoLink/Getty Images; **81** Lloyd Cluff/CORBIS; **83** Joseph Murphy; **84** Bedu Saini/AP Images; **86 87 88** S. Solum/PhotoLink/Getty Images; **89** (r)S. Solum/PhotoLink/Getty Images, (l)Getty Images; **90-91** Ralph White/CORBIS; **91** (inset)S. Solum/PhotoLink/Getty Images; **93** Stephen Frink/CORBIS; **94** Joseph Murphy; **96** A. Filis/AP Images; **97** Science Source/Photo Researchers; **98 99 100** S. Solum/PhotoLink/Getty Images; **101** (l)Scripps Inst Oceanography/Jupiter Images, (r)S. Solum/PhotoLink/Getty Images; **102-103** Andrew Syred/Photo Researchers, Inc.; **103** (inset)S. Solum/PhotoLink/Getty Images; **105** Kathy Atkinson/OSF/Animals Animals; **106** PHOTOTAKE Inc./Alamy Images; **107** Joseph Murphy; **110 111 112** S. Solum/PhotoLink/Getty Images; **113** (l)James Robinson/Animals Animals; (r)S. Solum/PhotoLink/Getty Images; **114** S. Solum/PhotoLink/Getty Images; **115** Comstock Images/Alamy Images; **116** Royalty-Free/CORBIS; **117** PhotoDisc/PunchStock; **Back Cover** Cartesia/Getty Images.